# EFFI~~ECTIVE~~ NONPROFIT MANAGEMENT

# EFFECTIVE NONPROFIT MANAGEMENT

## CONTEXT AND ENVIRONMENT

JOAN E. PYNES

*M.E.Sharpe*
Armonk, New York
London, England

**Library of Congress Cataloging-in-Publication Data**

Pynes, Joan.
  Effective nonprofit management : context and environment / by Joan E. Pynes.
    p. cm.
Includes bibliographical references and index.
ISBN 978-0-7656-3029-2 (hardcover: alk. paper)—ISBN 978-0-7656-3030-8 (pbk.: alk. paper)

  1. Nonprofit organizations—Management. I. Title.

  HD62.6.P96 2011
  658'.048—dc22                                                          2010046285

Printed in the United States of America

The paper used in this publication meets the minimum requirements of
American National Standard for Information Sciences
Permanence of Paper for Printed Library Materials,
ANSI Z 39.48-1984.

⊗

| IBT (c) | 10 | 9 | 8 | 7 | 6 | 5 | 4 | 3 | 2 | 1 |
| IBT (p) | 10 | 9 | 8 | 7 | 6 | 5 | 4 | 3 | 2 | 1 |

In memory and honor of my parents.

# Contents

# Preface

In 2008, 1,710,567 tax-exempt organizations, or 501(c)s, were registered with the federal government; public charity 501(c)(3)s were the largest portion at 1,186,915. That number does not take into account religious organizations or nonprofits that did not file an annual Internal Revenue Service (IRS) Form 990 (IRS 2008). The number of social welfare 501(c)(4)s had grown to 135,494. While the IRS numbers indicate an increase in the number of nonprofit organizations, newspaper articles from across the country are indicating that, due to the severe financial crisis, many nonprofits have been forced to discontinue operations or merge with other nonprofits offering similar or complementary services and programs.

Even before the current financial crisis, nonprofit managers, board members, and employees needed to address the challenges of changing social needs and priorities, new directions in public policy, and pressures for increased accountability. The environment in which nonprofits operated in the past had already begun to change. They had to compete with other nonprofits and for-profit agencies for government contracts and grants. The fund-raising environment had become more competitive as well.

If competition with other organizations is not distracting enough, the financial stress facing many state and local governments has prompted local governments to send property-tax bills to nonprofit organizations. It has been estimated that the property-tax exemption granted to nonprofit organizations costs local governments more than $1.5 billion annually (Lipman 2006).

As a result, more nonprofits are being asked to make payments in lieu of local taxes (PILOTs). Also, scrutiny has increased on the amount of charity care provided by nonprofit hospitals (Allen 2009; Bogan 2010; Goodnough 2009; King 2007; Ryan 2010; Slack 2008; Strom 2008; Wangsness 2010; Zook 2010).

Government and nonprofit organizations are facing many challenges.

They are confronted with tight budgets brought about by declines in tax revenues, declines in consumer spending, increases in unemployment, and federal government obligations in Iraq and Afghanistan, reducing the amount of federal dollars flowing to state and local government programs. Reductions in public dollars and private donations have required nonprofit organizations to lay off staff while demands for many services continue to increase. These changes have occurred simultaneously with increasing demands for efficient and effective services.

In many communities, cultural institutions are taking fiscal hits. In response to a weak economy, a drop in tourism, city budget cuts, and a decline in private contributions, museums, theaters, concert halls, opera companies, public gardens, and zoos are making adjustments in the number of performances, exhibitions, days of operation, and staff members (Associated Press 2009; Banjo 2010; Banjo and Kalita 2010; Fountain 2009; Pogrebin 2009; Royce 2009; Trescott 2010; Viera 2010). Nonprofit agencies are impacted by economic uncertainty in other ways. Individuals who have been or might be laid off are less inclined to spend dollars on cultural activities than more securely employed people, exacerbating the financial pressures on these already stressed agencies.

Uncertain financial times cause citizens to focus more on the performance of the public and nonprofit sectors. People with less money to spend want assurances that their tax dollars are spent wisely and without waste. This is especially true given the revelations of how some of the money raised by nonprofits does not go to provide programs and services. Stories about inflated executive salaries, misappropriated funds, double-counting donations, and inflating membership numbers have had an impact on the confidence many donors or potential donors have in nonprofits.

Tough financial times provoke greater scrutiny of an agency's performance. The apparent lack of governance by nonprofit directors and boards has led to a demand for increased accountability by federal and state oversight agencies such as the Internal Revenue Service (IRS), Senate Finance Committee, and state attorney general offices, but also by funders and donors. Transparency in operations and performance outcomes and improvements in internal governance are expected.

Greater emphasis is being placed on social enterprise activities. Nonprofits are expected to diversify their revenue streams and eliminate their reliance on public monies or foundation grants. Those in leadership positions are increasingly being expected to understand, supervise, and implement finance strategies and social marketing.

It is anticipated that a leadership crisis in nonprofit management is impending. A significant number of executive directors/CEOs will be retiring shortly, amid concerns that there are not enough individuals qualified to become the next generation of leaders. The recent economic meltdown has slowed the retirement of many individuals whose retirement accounts lost money, but at some point, they will be leaving the workforce. Their replacements will need to understand the context in which they will be operating, and they will need enhanced administrative and management skills.

Changes in information technology and automation led to the restructuring of many nonprofit agencies. Advances in technology have enabled employees to work from their homes, provided opportunities for more flexible work hours, and increased the employment options for disabled individuals. Information technology is being used not only to automate routine tasks, but also to restructure and integrate service delivery procedures and programs. Many government agencies and foundations now require nonprofits to submit grant proposals and annual performance reports through the Internet. The Internet is also increasingly being used for fund-raising and advocacy activities, often requiring greater technology skills from nonprofit staff and upgrades of computer hardware and software.

Nonprofit agencies must be flexible and attuned to the needs of society. They must also seek better ways to meet the expectations held by citizens, clients, funding sources, foundations, elected officials, boards of directors, interest groups, and the media. They need to understand the role that advocacy and lobbying play in influencing the public policies that affect them. They also need to understand where the money that funds their activities comes from and how to be better financial stewards.

**Purpose and Audience**

While there are a number of excellent books on nonprofit management, there are some critical topics that nonprofit administrators, board members, and program managers need to be familiar with and that have not been addressed. This book covers accountability; board governance; intergovernmental relations and public policy; financial management; organization effectiveness and performance measurement; human re-

sources management; and nonprofit advocacy. Many of these topics are covered in other books but not placed in a broader context.

The purpose of this book is to introduce the reader to issues affecting nonprofit management. It is also intended to be a companion to other sources of information such as single-topic books (examples of such topics include strategic planning, human resources management, financial management, board development, fund-raising, grantsmanship), case studies, books on nonprofit management activities, and books addressing the current research in the field.

This book seeks to provide the context in which nonprofit organizations operate. Many nonprofit administrators perform tasks but do not understand the reasoning behind them, nor do they understand their organizations' context. As a result, they are not discerning users of information. Many of the changes that nonprofits are facing are outside of their control. However, understanding how changes in the external environment impact internal operations and constituent and community services is critical. Too many nonprofit executives and board members have been like deer caught in the headlights of oncoming cars. Nonprofits need proactive leadership. Nonprofit administrators need to understand how changes in the external environment impact the administration and management of agencies. Understanding the context is necessary for effective and professional administration of nonprofit organizations.

## Overview of Contents

Chapter 1 explains what independent nonprofit organizations are, how society has changed, and the management implications for those changes. Chapter 2 addresses why accountability has become such an important topic for nonprofit organizations; it discusses the impending changes on the IRS Form 990, ethical behavior, and the recommendations from the Panel on the Nonprofit Sector's 2005, 2006, and 2007 reports to Congress.

Chapter 3 discusses board governance. It explains the responsibilities of a board of directors and includes research findings that identify elements for effective board service. Chapter 4 discusses the importance for nonprofit administrators to understand intergovernmental relations and public policy. For the most part (there are exceptions), nonprofit employees do not understand the complex intergovernmental environment in which they operate nor do they understand the relationships between local, state, and federal policy, and how the public policies that affect them are made. Chapter 5 discusses the different sources of revenue that fund nonprofits. Social enterprise activities to generate revenue are also discussed. Improving agency effectiveness and the performance of programs through performance management is presented in chapter 6. Human resource management issues are discussed in chapter 7—topics include when discrimination on the basis of religion is permitted during the selection process, recruiting and managing volunteers, as well as the leadership deficit that nonprofits may experience when incumbent employees retire. The difference between advocacy and lobbying is explained in chapter 8 and the book concludes with expectations for the future.

## Acknowledgments

I am grateful to Harry M. Briggs and the editors at M.E. Sharpe for their support of this project. I would like to express appreciation to my sister, Robyn Pynes Roach, and my husband, Mike McNaughton, for their consistent encouragement and support. Special acknowledgment goes to my husband for his sense of humor, editing assistance, and agility in sidestepping stacks of books, journals, and papers. To the camp group— looking forward to another twenty-five years.

## References

Allen, S. (2009). Hospitals not paying fair share. *Boston Globe,* January 21. www.boston.com/news/local/massachusetts/articles/2009/01/21/hospitals_not_paying_fair_share_group_says/.

Associated Press (2009). Economic woes felt at zoos, aquariums. *Tampa Tribune,* January 14. www2.tbo.com/content/2009/jan/14/na-economic-woes-felt-at-zoos-aquariums/c_1/.

Banjo, S. (2010). Hit by the downturn, museums seek bailouts. *Wall Street Journal,* May 20. http://online.wsj.com/article/SB10001424052748703691804575254321564633624.html.

Banjo, S., and S.M. Kalita (2010). Once robust charity sector hit with mergers, closings. *Wall Street Journal,* February 1. http://online.wsj.com/article/SB10001424052748704586504574654404227641232.html.

Bogan, J. (2010). St. Louis officials weigh asking nonprofits to chip in for services. *St. Louis Post-Dispatch,* April 7. www.stltoday.com/news/local/metro/article_0bcf7711–92ed-5327–80c6–926b887f9b18.html?print=1.

Fountain, H. (2009). In zoo, it's man vs. beast. *New York Times,* March 19, F28.

Goodnough, A. (2009). Slump revives town-gown divide across U.S. *New York Times,* May 9, A1.

Internal Revenue Service (2008). *Data Book, 2008*. www.irs.gov/pub/irs-soi/08databk.pdf.

King, R. (2007). Lawmakers consider fees for nonprofits. *Indianapolis Star*, December 2, wwww.indystar.com/A27.

Lipman, H. (2006). The value of a tax break. *The Chronicle of Philanthropy*. November 23. http://philanthrophy.com.

Pogrebin, R. (2009). New York's local museums feel the pinch. *New York Times*, March 19, SPG6.

Royce, G. (2009). Walker trims budget by $2 million this year, next. *Minneapolis-St. Paul Star Tribune*, March 17. www.startribune.com/templates/Print_This_Story?sid=41334892.

Ryan, A. (2010). City asks exempt sector for help: Task force readies payment formula; Some nonprofits balk at proposals. *Boston Globe*, April 6. www.boston.com/news/local/massachusetts/articles/2010/04/06/city_asks_exempt_sector_for_help/.

Slack, D. (2008). Tax hunt targets exempt groups: City to study nonprofits. *Boston Globe,* December 9. www.boston.com/news/local/massachusetts/articles/2008/12/09/tax_hunt_targets_exempt_groups/.

Strom, S. (2008). Tax exemptions of charities face new challenges. *New York Times*, May 26. www.nytimes.com/2008/05/26/us/26tax.html.

Trescott, J. (2010). The National Arts Index, a new survey by Americans for the arts, paints a troubling picture for arts organizations. *Washington Post*, January 21, C02.

Viera, L. (2010). Art Institute lays off some 65 staffers. *Chicago Tribune*, May 24. http://articles.chicagotribune.com/2010–05–24/entertainment/ct-live-0525-art-institute-layoffs-20100524_1_modern-wing-museum-spokeswoman-erin-hogan-art-institute.

Wangsness, L. (2010). Strapped towns tax Catholic properties: Church forced to pay for shuttered buildings. *Boston Globe*, May 31. www.boston.com/news/local/massachusetts/articles/2010/05/31/boston_area_communities_taxing_closed_catholic_properties/.

Zook, S. (2010). Despite city shortfall, no PILOT aid. *Temple News*, April 20. http://temple-news.com/2010/04/20/despite-city-shortfall-no-pilot-aid/.

# EFFECTIVE
# NONPROFIT
# MANAGEMENT

# 1

# The Independent Nonprofit Sector

More than 1.5 million nonprofits registered with the Internal Revenue Service in 2008 (National Center for Charitable Statistics (NCCS) 2010). However, that figure is believed to be understated, because nonprofits with less than $5,000 in annual revenues and religious congregations are not required to register with the IRS. The Internal Revenue Code defines more than thirty kinds of tax-exempt organizations. Thirty of them fall under the Section 501(c) designation, while the rest have a different numerical designation, such as Section 527 Political Organizations or Section 494(a)(2) Split Interest Trust designation. Table 1.1 lists the different types of associations, corporations, and trusts that can qualify for federal tax exemption.

Typically when we think of nonprofit organizations, we think of those we are familiar with or that are written about in the local newspapers or featured on TV; the United Way of America, the Society for the Prevention of the Cruelty to Animals (SPCA), the Boys & Girls Clubs, Big Brothers and Big Sisters, St. Jude's Hospital in Memphis, the Metropolitan Museum of Art (MOMA), the Catholic Church, as well as smaller tax-exempt organizations that operate in our communities and provide community and social support such as Meals on Wheels, community arts groups, community service clubs, sport leagues, and parent-teacher associations (PTAs). These organizations fall under Section 501(c)(3) and are *public charity* nonprofit organizations. The largest category of tax-exempt nonprofit organizations is public charity. Human service, education, health-care, cultural, and recreation nonprofits fall in this category.

The Sierra Club, the American Civil Liberties Union (ACLU), and the League of Women Voters are 501(c)(4) *social welfare* nonprofit organizations. As defined by the IRS, social welfare organizations "further the common good and general welfare of the people of a community (such as bringing about civic betterment and social improvements" (IRS 2008).

3

Table 1.1

## IRS Organization Reference Chart

| Section of 1986 Code | Description of organization | General nature of activities | Application form number | Annual return required to be filed | Contributions allowable |
|---|---|---|---|---|---|
| 501(c)(1) | Corporations organized under act of Congress (including federal credit unions) | Instrumentalities of the United States | No form | None | Yes, if made for exclusively public purposes |
| 501(c)(2) | Title holding corporation for exempt organization | Hold title to property of an exempt organization | 1024 | 990[1] or 990EZ[8] | No[2] |
| 501(c)(3) | Religious, educational, charitable, scientific, literary, testing for public safety, to foster national or international amateur sports competition, or prevention of cruelty to children or animals organizations | Activities of nature implied by description of class of organization | 1023 | 990[1] or 990EZ,[8] or 990-PF | Yes, generally |
| 501(c)(4) | Civic leagues, social welfare organizations, and local associations of employees | Promotion of community welfare; charitable, educational, or recreational | 1024 | 990[1] or 990EZ[8] | No, generally[2,3] |
| 501(c)(5) | Labor, agricultural, and horticultural organizations | Educational or instructive, the purpose being to improve conditions of work and to improve products of efficiency | 1024 | 990[1] or 990EZ[8] | No[2] |
| 501(c)(6) | Business leagues, chambers of commerce, real estate boards, etc. | Improvement of business conditions of one or more lines of business | 1024 | 990[1] or 990EZ[8] | No[2] |
| 501(c)(7) | Social and recreational clubs | Pleasure, recreation, social activities | 1024 | 990[1] or 990EZ[8] | No[2] |
| 501(c)(8) | Fraternal beneficiary societies and associations | Lodge providing for payment of life, sickness, accident, or other benefits to members | 1024 | 990[1] or 990EZ[8] | Yes, if for certain Sec. 501(c)(3) purposes |

| | | | | |
|---|---|---|---|---|
| 501(c)(9) | Voluntary employees' beneficiary associations | Providing for payment of life, sickness, accident, or other benefits to members | 1024 | 990[1] or 990EZ[8] | No[2] |
| 501(c)(10) | Domestic fraternal societies and associations | Lodge devoting its net earnings to charitable, fraternal, and other specified purposes. No life, sickness, or accident benefits to members | 1024 | 990[1] or 990EZ[8] | Yes, if for certain Sec. 501(c)(3) purposes |
| 501(c)(11) | Teachers' retirement fund associations | Teachers' association for payment of retirement benefits | No form[6] | 990[1] or 990EZ[8] | No[2] |
| 501(c)(12) | Benevolent life insurance associations, mutual ditch or irrigation companies, mutual or cooperative telephone companies, etc. | Activities of a mutually beneficial nature similar to those implied by description of class of organization | 1024 | 990[1] or 990EZ[8] | No[2] |
| 501(c)(13) | Cemetery companies | Burials and incidental activities | 1024 | 990[1] or 990EZ[8] | Yes, generally |
| 501(c)(14) | State-chartered credit unions, mutual reserve funds | Loans to members | No form[6] | 990[1] or 990EZ[8] | No[2] |
| 501(c)(15) | Mutual insurance companies or associations | Provides insurance to members substantially at cost | 1024 | 990[1] or 990EZ[8] | No[2] |
| 501(c)(16) | Cooperative organizations to finance crop operations | Finances crop operations in conjunction with activities of a marketing or purchasing association | No form[6] | 990[1] or 990EZ[8] | No[2] |
| 501(c)(17) | Supplemental unemployment benefit trusts | Provides for payment of supplemental unemployment compensation benefits | 1024 | 990[1] or 990EZ[8] | No[2] |
| 501(c)(18) | Employee-funded pension trust (created before June 25, 1959) | Payment of benefits under a pension plan funded by employees | No form[6] | 990[1] or 990EZ[8] | No[2] |
| 501(c)(19) | Post or organization of past or present members of the armed forces | Activities implied by nature of organization | 1024 | 990[1] or 990EZ[8] | No, generally[7] |

*(continued)*

Table 1.1 (continued)

| Section of 1986 Code | Description of organization | General nature of activities | Application form number | Annual return required to be filed | Contributions allowable |
|---|---|---|---|---|---|
| 501(c)(21) | Black lung benefit trusts | Funded by coal mine operators to satisfy their liability for disability or death due to black lung diseases | No form[6] | 990-BL | No[4] |
| 501(c)(22) | Withdrawal liability payment fund | Provides funds to meet the liability of employers withdrawing from a multi-employer pension fund | No form[6] | 990 or 990EZ[8] | No[5] |
| 501(c)(23) | Veterans organization (created before 1880) | Provides insurance and other benefits to veterans | No form[6] | 990 or 990EZ[8] | No, generally[7] |
| 501(c)(25) | Title-holding corporations or trusts with multiple parents | Holding title and paying over income from property to thirty-five or fewer parents or beneficiaries | 1024 | 990 or 990EZ | No |
| 501(c)(26) | State-sponsored organization providing health coverage for high-risk individuals | Provides health care coverage to high-risk individuals | No form[6] | 990[1] or 990EZ[8] | No |
| 501(c)(27) | State-sponsored workers' compensation reinsurance organization | Reimburses members for losses under workers' compensation acts | No form[6] | 990[1] or 990EZ[8] | No |
| 501(c)(28) | National Railroad Retirement Investment Trust | Manages and invests the assets of the Railroad Retirement Account | No form | None | No |
| 501(d) | Religious and apostolic associations | Regular business activities; communal religious community | No form | 1065[9] | No[2] |
| 501(e) | Cooperative hospital service organizations | Performs cooperative services for hospitals | 1023 | 990[1] or 990EZ[8] | Yes |

| 501(f) | Cooperative service organizations of operating educational organizations | 1023 | 990[1] or 990EZ[8] | Yes |
|---|---|---|---|---|
| 501(k) | Child-care organizations | 1023 | 990 or 990EZ[8] | Yes |
| 501(n) | Charitable risk pools | 1023 | 990[1] or 990EZ[8] | Yes |
| 501(q) | Credit Counseling Organization | 1023 | 1023[12] | No |
| 521(a) | Farmers' cooperative associations | 1028 | 990-C | No |
| 527 | Political organizations | 8871 | 1120-POL[10] 990[1] or 990EZ[8] | No |

*Source:* IRS Publication 557, www.irs.gov/pub/irs-pdf/p.557.pdf (pp. 65–66).

[1] For exceptions to the filing requirement, see chapter 2 and the form instructions.

[2] An organization exempt under a subsection of Code Section 501 other than 501(c)(3) may establish a charitable fund, contributions to which are deductible. Such a fund must itself meet the requirements of Section 501(c)(3) and the related notice requirements of Section 508(a).

[3] Contributions to volunteer fire companies and similar organizations are deductible, but only if made for exclusively public purposes.

[4] Deductible as a business expense to the extent allowed by Code Section 192.

[5] Deductible as a business expense to the extent allowed by Code Section 194A.

[6] Application is by letter to the address shown on Form 8718. A copy of the organizing document should be attached, and the letter should be signed by an officer.

[7] Contributions to these organizations are deductible only if 90 percent or more of the organization's members are war veterans.

[8] For limits on the use of Form 990EZ, see chapter 2 and the general instructions for Form 990EZ (or Form 990).

[9] Although the organization files a partnership return, all distributions are deemed dividends. The members are not entitled to *pass-through* treatment of the organization's income or expenses.

[10] Form 1120-POL is required only if the organization has taxable income as defined in Code Section 527(c).

[11] Application procedures not yet determined.

[12] Use Form 1024 if applying for recognition under Code section 501(c)(4).

There are other kinds of tax-exempt organizations as well. Labor unions and organizations such as the AFL-CIO, Teamsters, Fraternal Order of Police, and Service Employees International Union (SEIU) are 501(c)(5) tax-exempt organizations, and chambers of commerce and some professional organizations are referred to as business leagues and fall under 501(c)(6). IRS Publication 557 provides an explanation of the different kinds of 501(c) organizations (IRS 2010).

The *nonprofit sector* is the collective name used to describe organizations that are not government or private for-profit organizations. They are created by private interests, are privately owned, and do not seek profits. Any surplus revenues are invested back into the nonprofit instead of being paid out to shareholders or private owners. Nonprofit organizations are chartered by each state and are conferred special tax-exempt status on their federal income taxes by the Internal Revenue Code (IRC). Nonprofits exempt from federal income tax are typically granted exemptions from states and local income taxes as well. State and local governments may also grant nonprofits exemptions from property and sales taxes. The reason that nonprofits are tax-exempt is that they mitigate many of the responsibilities of government. Day-care centers, recreation, cultural and educational programs, and social and health-care facilities provide services that government might be required to supply. By offering tax exemptions, government supports the work of nonprofits. Sometimes professional associations and social welfare organizations do not meet local and state exemptions. Nonprofits are not exempt from paying payroll taxes for employees, and they are also required to pay taxes on income from activities that are unrelated to their mission.

To be recognized as a nonprofit, an organization must possess the following general characteristics:

1. It is specifically designated as a nonprofit when organized.
2. Profits or assets may not be divided among corporate members, officers, or directors in the manner of corporate dividends.
3. It may lawfully pursue only such purposes as are permitted for such organizations by statutes (Oleck 1988).

Internal Revenue Code 501(c) lists the different types of associations, corporations, and trusts that can qualify for federal tax exemption.

The focus of this book is on the *independent nonprofit sector*, nonprofit organizations that are incorporated to provide a public benefit. This chapter will provide a brief overview of the nonprofit sector in general and will answer the following questions:

- What is the nonprofit sector?
- What are some differences between 501(c)(3) and 501(c)(4) non-profit organizations?
- How are economic challenges affecting nonprofit management?
- How are technology changes affecting nonprofit management?
- How are social changes affecting nonprofit management?
- How will the changes in the legal environments affect nonprofit management?

The largest nonprofit classification is 501(c)(3). These organizations are referred to as *public charities*. Charitable nonprofits are private organizations that serve a public purpose. They operate under a nondistribution component, which prohibits the distribution of profits or residual earnings to individuals who control the entity—excess revenues are invested back into the nonprofit and are not paid as dividends to individual shareholders. Because of this restriction, it is believed that they possess a greater moral authority and concern for the public interest than private for-profit organizations do. Nonprofits often perform public tasks that have been delegated to them by the state or perform tasks for which there is a demand that neither government nor for-profit organizations provide. They offer a variety of services, such as providing occupational training or counseling services to the disadvantaged, providing medical services, developing recreational programs, providing cultural and educational activities, preserving the environment, and funding medical research. Donations to 501(c)(3) public charity nonprofits are deductible from the taxes that individuals and corporations owe on their personal and business income taxes because nonprofits provide a public benefit, and the tax deductions encourage donations.

Nonprofits are thought to be more flexible than government agencies. They can experiment with new programs, responding more quickly to new social needs. Instead of getting involved in new or controversial programs, government often gives money to nonprofit agencies to provide services. Nonprofits get financial support, and clients receive services. Government, through the conditions it places on agencies that receive public funds, still has some influence but can quickly disassociate itself from programs when things go wrong. There are often certain societal needs that may be too expensive to be provided on a private for-profit basis. Therefore, in the United States, both government and the nonprofit sector provide certain services whose costs exceed their market value (Douglas 1983; O'Neil 1989; Salamon 1999; Weisbrod 1997).

The IRS defines a public charity as an organization that normally receives a substantial portion of its total income directly or indirectly from the general public or government. In other words, it can demonstrate that it has broad support, rather than funding from an individual source. Other 501(c) classifications derive most of their money from their members and primarily serve the interests of their members. Because of their public serving nature, individual and corporate donations to 501(c)(3) public charity nonprofits are deductible from taxable federal income tax.

Private foundations are also 501(c)(3) nonprofits but are not considered to be public charities. Foundations receive the majority of their money from a few donors. One company, one family, or one person can start a foundation. Tax treatment of private foundations is different from that of public charities. The tax deductions permitted to individual donors for gifts to private foundations are more limited. The investment earnings of private foundations are subject to a tax on their net investment earnings, and the foundations are required to spend at least 5 percent of their investment assets each year. Foundations are usually funding intermediaries that do not operate their own programs but make gifts or grants to other nonprofits that do. However, a few foundations like the Carnegie Endowment for International Peace and the Getty Trust are operating foundations, which means that they use their resources to implement their own programs rather than make grants to other nonprofits. Table 1.2 indicates the growth in the number of nonprofit organizations in the United States between 1998 and 2008. Included in Table 1.2 are 501(c) (3) nonprofits, public charities and private foundations, and other 501(c) nonprofit organizations.

The National Taxonomy of Exempt Organizations, developed by the National Center for Charitable Statistics, provides a classification system for public charity nonprofit organizations. There are ten major groups, twenty-six categories, and over four hundred subcategories. Table 1.3 illustrates the major groups and how many of them existed in each major group for 2007.

Social welfare nonprofits, often referred to as *advocacy organizations*, are another classification of nonprofits that are public serving. The American Civil Liberties Union, the National Rifle Association (NRA), and the Sierra Club are examples. They cannot receive tax-deductible gifts, they engage in more lobbying activities, and they can advocate for specific issues. Along with 501(c)(3) nonprofits, they constitute what is referred to as the *independent sector* (Weitzman et al. 2002). Many 501(c)(4) nonprofits have affiliated 501(c)(3) nonprofits to assist with fund-raising, and they often establish foundations, since donations to them are not tax-deductible. And many 501(c)(3) nonprofits have affiliated 501(c)(4) organizations to engage in lobbying and advocacy activities, because 501(c)(3) nonprofits have more restrictive limits on their lobbying and political advocacy activities than 501(c)(4) nonprofits do.

The Alliance for Justice (www.afj.org) provides live as well as online workshops, and publishes booklets and fact sheets on the permissible advocacy activities for 501(c)(3) and 501(c)(4) organizations.

## Nonprofit Contributions to Society

In *The Resilient Sector: The State of Nonprofit America* (2002), Lester M. Salamon identifies five critical roles and functions performed by the nonprofit sector: providing services, providing advocacy activities and identifying problems, allowing for individual and group expressions, building social capital and engagement in community building, and acting as a value guardian.

In their *service provision roles*, nonprofits often exist as a first line of defense or provide a flexible means through which individuals concerned about a social or economic problem can begin to respond. Nonprofits have been instrumental in identifying and addressing unmet needs. Nonprofits were at the forefront of providing assistance to AIDS victims, hospice care, emergency shelter for the homeless, food pantries, drug abuse treatment efforts, and so on. Today, nonprofits deliver much of the hospital care, higher education, social services, cultural enter-tainment, employment and training, low-income housing, community development, and emergency aid services available in the United States (Salamon 2002, 9–10).

In their *advocacy roles*, nonprofits identify problems and bring them to public attention. They also protect basic human rights and give voice to a wide assortment of social, political, environmental, ethnic, and community interests and concerns. Social movements such as antislavery, women's suffrage, civil rights, pro-environment, antiwar, women's rights, gay rights, and conservative movements began in the nonprofit sector. Nonprofits have been able to mobilize public attention on societal problems and needs,

12

Table 1.2

## Number of Nonprofit Organizations in the United States, 1998–2008

| | 1998 | | 2008 | | |
|---|---|---|---|---|---|
| | No. of orgs. | % of all orgs. | No. of orgs. | % of all orgs. | % change |
| **All Nonprofit Organizations** | 1,158,031 | 100.0 | 1,536,134 | 100.0 | 32.7 |
| 501(C)(3) public charities | 596,160 | 51.5 | 974,337 | 63.4 | 63.4 |
| 501(C)(3) private foundations | 70,480 | 6.1 | 115,340 | 7.5 | 63.6 |
| Other 501(c) nonprofit organizations | 491,391 | 42.4 | 446,457 | 29.1 | -9.1 |
| Small community groups and partnerships, etc. | Unknown | NA | Unknown | NA | NA |
| **501(C)(3) public charities registered with the IRS (including registered congregations)** | 596,160 | 51.5 | 974,337 | 63.4 | 63.4 |
| Reporting public charities | 231,625 | 20.0 | 483,779 | 31.5 | 108.9 |
| Operating public charities | 201,175 | 17.4 | 426,033 | 27.7 | 111.8 |
| Supporting public charities | 30,450 | 2.6 | 57,746 | 3.8 | 89.6 |
| Nonreporting, or with less than $25,000 in gross receipts | 364,535 | 31.57 | 490,558 | 31.9 | 34.6 |
| Congregations (about half are registered with IRS)* | — | 0.0 | 385,874 | 25.1 | NA |
| **501(C)(3) private foundations** | 70,480 | 6.1 | 115,340 | 7.5 | 63.6 |
| Private grant-making (nonoperating) foundations | 67,625 | 5.8 | 110,099 | 7.2 | 62.8 |
| Private operating foundations | 2,855 | 0.2 | 5,241 | 0.3 | 83.6 |

| Other 501(c) nonprofit organizations | 491,391 | 42.4 | 446,457 | 29.1 | −9.1 |
|---|---|---|---|---|---|
| Civic leagues, social welfare organizations, etc. | 125,504 | 10.8 | 110,924 | 7.2 | −11.6 |
| Fraternal beneficiary societies | 103,065 | 8.9 | 78,109 | 5.1 | −24.2 |
| Business leagues, chambers of commerce, etc. | 69,734 | 6.0 | 71,887 | 4.7 | 3.1 |
| Labor, agricultural, horticultural organizations | 61,444 | 5.3 | 55,629 | 3.6 | −9.5 |
| Social and recreational clubs | 56,452 | 4.9 | 55,838 | 3.6 | −1.1 |
| Post or organization of war veterans | 34,272 | 3.0 | 32,592 | 2.1 | −4.9 |
| All other nonprofit organizations | 40,920 | 3.5 | 41,478 | 2.7 | 1.4 |

*Source:* IRS Business Master File 04/2009 (with modifications by the National Center for Charitable Statistics at the Urban Institute to exclude foreign and governmental organizations).

*Note:* Excludes out-of-scope organizations.

*The number of congregations is from the website of American Church Lists (http://list.infousa.com/acl.htm), 2004. These numbers are excluded from the totals for the state since approximately half of the congregations are included under registered public charities.

Reprinted with the permission of the Urban Institute. NCCS website, Number of Nonprofit Organizations in the United States, 1998–2008. Located http://nccsdataweb.urban.org/PubApps/profile1.php?state=us.

Table 1.3

**National Taxonomy of Exempt Entities: Broad Categories**

| Major Group | |
|---|---|
| Arts, Culture, and Humanities | A |
| Education | B |
| Environment and Animals | C, D |
| Health | E, F, G, H |
| Human Services | I, J, K, L, M, N, O, P |
| International, Foreign Affairs | Q |
| Public, Societal Benefit | R, S, T, U, V, W |
| Religion-Related | X |
| Mutual/Membership Benefit | Y |
| Unknown, Unclassified | Z |

| NTEE Major Group | | Number of Organizations |
|---|---|---|
| A. | Arts, Culture, and Humanities | 38,771 |
| B. | Education | 64,363 |
| C. | Environmental Quality, Protection, and Beautification | 8,086 |
| D. | Animal-Related | 7,207 |
| E. | Health | 23,553 |
| F. | Mental Health, Crisis Intervention | 9,197 |
| G. | Diseases, Disorders, Medical Disciplines | 8,616 |
| H. | Medical Research | 2,226 |
| I. | Crime, Legal-Related | 6,099 |
| J. | Employment, Job-Related | 4,152 |
| K. | Food, Agriculture, and Nutrition | 3,493 |
| L. | Housing and Shelter | 17,257 |
| M. | Public Safety, Disaster Preparedness and Relief | 6,314 |
| N. | Recreation and Sports | 29,513 |
| O. | Youth Development | 8,380 |
| P. | Human Services | 43,205 |
| Q. | International, Foreign Affairs, and National Security | 6,793 |
| R. | Civil Rights, Social Action, and Advocacy | 2,281 |
| S. | Community Improvement and Capacity Building | 16,753 |
| T. | Philanthropy, Voluntarism, and Grantmaking Foundations | 16,401 |
| U. | Science and Technology | 2,196 |
| V. | Social Science | 865 |
| W. | Public and Societal Benefit | 3,766 |
| X. | Religion-Related | 22,400 |
| Y. | Mutual/Membership Benefit | 883 |
| Z. | Unknown | 927 |
| | Total | 353,697 |

*Source:* NCCS website, 501(c)(3) Public Charities Core File 2008. Reprinted with the permission of the Urban Institute.

give voice to unrepresented people and points of view, and integrate these perspectives into social and political life (ibid., 10).

Through their *expressive role*, nonprofits contribute to the social and cultural vitality of community life. Opera companies, symphonies, museums, zoos, churches, synagogues, mosques, book clubs, and fraternal societies are typically nonprofits. Artistic, cultural, ethnic, social, and recreational expressions are fostered through nonprofits (ibid.).

Nonprofits are also important in creating *social capital* and *community building*. They serve to establish connections among individuals who become involved in associations that carry over into political and economic life (ibid., 10–11).

Lastly, nonprofits often serve as *value guardians*, because they help to nurture and sustain the values and behaviors of individual initiative for the public good. Through nonprofits, individuals can take the initiative to advance the well-being of others (ibid., 11).

## Nonprofit Administrative Structures

Despite their diverse purposes, nonprofits have similar administrative structures. A nonprofit's administrative structure is governed by its bylaws, internal documents that typically define most operational and management policies. Bylaws regulate the organization's procedures and internal practices, as well as define the duties, powers, and limitations of the directors, officers, and other agents. Like all important documents, the bylaws should be reviewed periodically and updated.

Nonprofit organizations themselves possess legal power. Directors are elected or appointed to the board and are authorized to manage and direct the affairs of the organization. They act on behalf of the organization but do not have ownership powers within it; their control is managerial and proprietary. They are free only to change policies and short-range purposes unless the charter or bylaws permit the directors to change the fundamental purpose or policies. Many states permit the delegation of direct authority to committees to study and make recommendations about some matter or to manage routine affairs.

## The Present Context for Nonprofit Management

Nonprofits, like for-profits and public organizations, are facing many economic, legal, technical, and social challenges.

## Economic Challenges

Nonprofits are facing severe economic challenges. Declines in public revenues mean less support for many nonprofit organizations. Uncertain financial times place additional stresses on them. Increased unemployment often requires the expansion of food assistance, medical aid, job training, rent assistance, or retraining services. These services are typically provided by nonprofit agencies, which must absorb an increase in demand for services without increasing their staffs, while possibly facing layoffs due to decreases in government funding. Low-income residents are dependent on a variety of services such as those involving housing, medical care, food, unemployment benefits, transportation, and utility bills. This increased need forces states and local governments to use even more of their already sparse budgets toward providing these services.

The housing crisis and recession have resulted in lower property taxes, sales taxes, and income taxes, as well as tourist taxes and other revenues. Increased unemployment has led to a larger number of homeless families, greater demands on area food banks, and an increasing health-care crisis (Bosman 2009; Connolly 2009; Eckholm 2009; Goldstein 2009; Lampman 2009; Stobbe 2009; Vestal 2009; White et al., 2009).

The *Fiscal Survey of the States: June 2010*, a report prepared by the National Governors Association and the National Associations of State Budget Officers, notes that fiscal 2010 presented the most difficult financial management for states since the Great Depression. The recession reduced tax revenues from every revenue source. The report anticipates that state revenues will remain low through 2011 and 2012 (Husch et al. 2010). The federal stimulus money that states received this year is not likely to be forthcoming next year, which could mean additional stress on state and local government budgets and the funding that nonprofits receive from those sources (Anderson 2010; Couloumbis 2010).

The National Council of Nonprofits (2010) prepared a special report, *State Budget Crises: Ripping the Safety Net Held by Nonprofits*, which identified three critical financial threats to nonprofits: governments are cutting funds for essential programs, governments are reducing or withholding payments, and governments are imposing new taxes or new fees or are seeking payments in lieu of taxes (PILOTS) on nonprofits.

Nonprofit agencies are affected by economic uncertainty in other ways. Individuals who have been or might be laid off are less inclined than more securely employed people to spend money on cultural activities. *Giving*

*USA 2010: The Annual Report on Philanthropy for the Year 2009* (2010) found that total charitable giving fell 3.6 percent in 2009. This was the steepest decline in current dollars since Giving USA began its annual reports in 1956 (p. vi). The report cautions that the decline in giving may not be reflective of all nonprofits and across all of the subsectors. Individuals provided 75 percent of the giving, followed by foundations at 13 percent, bequests 8 percent, and corporations 4 percent. Religion-related nonprofits received the greatest percentage of giving, 33 percent, followed by education at 13 percent, gifts to grant-making foundations at 10 percent, unallocated giving at 10 percent, human services at 9 percent, public-society benefit at 8 percent, health at 7 percent, arts, culture, and humanities at 4 percent, international affairs at 3 percent, environment/animals at 2 percent, and foundation grants to individuals at 1 percent.

Almost daily, news articles address the financial troubles of museums, orchestras, and other cultural institutions across the country (Healy 2009; Fountain 2009; Pogrebin 2009; Royce 2009; Sheets 2009). Foundation assets have declined by nearly $150 billion (Strom 2009c), and some foundations and United Ways have refocused their donations to address the most pressing needs (Azam 2009; Glader 2008), while still other grantmakers are raising their payouts, reducing administrative costs, and cutting programs (McGill and Lawrence 2009). Research by the Nonprofit Finance Fund found that only 12 percent of nonprofits surveyed expect to break even this year; just 16 percent anticipate being able to cover their operating expenses in 2009 and 1010; 31 percent do not have enough operating cash in hand to cover more than one month of expenses, and another 31 percent have less than three months' worth; 52 percent of the respondents expect the recession to have a long-term or permanent negative effect on their organizations; and 93 percent of organizations that provide essential services anticipate an increase in demand in 2009 (Nonprofit Finance Fund 2009). Companies such as Northrop Grumman, General Motors, Embarq, CSX Corporations, Procter & Gamble, Weyerhaeuser, IndyMac, Pfizer, and R.H. Donnelley have either discontinued their matching gift contributions to nonprofits or reduced the matching ratio (Banjo 2009).

Unable to cope with the decline in revenues, some nonprofits are closing or merging with other nonprofits, and in some cases seeking bankruptcy protection (Greenwell and Harris 2009; Kostrze 2008; Sataline 2008; Strom 2009a. The Wall Street fraud and credit crises have taken away many previous options (Spector 2008; Strom 2008,

2009a). Middle-income Americans are increasingly concerned over jobs, health insurance, pensions, housing, and income security as well. Wage and salary raises have not kept up with increases in housing, gasoline, food, education, and insurance. Residents concerned about their living expenses tend to keep a closer eye on government spending and want tax relief. At the same time, state and local governments are facing budget deficits and are forced to make budget cuts. Problems with the housing markets and foreclosures (leading to reduced property taxes), reductions in sales taxes due to declines in consumer confidence, and increasing unemployment rates have led to reductions in spending, so state and local revenues are falling (Prah 2009). This has resulted in nonprofits' reducing services. In New York City at least fifty senior centers are expected to close, while in Everett, Washington, the YMCA lost a city contract worth $131,700, eleven homeless shelters in Seattle may close, and South Jersey Legal Services will be laying off one-third of its employees (Chen 2010; Press of Atlantic City Staff 2010; Rathburn 2010; L.C. Williams 2010).

There is a greater emphasis on social enterprise activities as well. Nonprofits are expected to diversify their revenue streams and eliminate their reliance on public monies or foundation grants. The leadership of nonprofit organizations must understand, supervise, and implement financial strategies so the agencies remain viable. Tough financial times also provoke a greater scrutiny on performance outcomes and indicators of effectiveness.

There are also new corporate forms that recognize social businesses whose primary business is service and not profits. Low-profit limited liability corporations (L3Cs) and B corporations are recognized by some states and local government. They are run like a business and are profitable, but their primary aim is to provide a social benefit often referred to as a double bottom line. Social benefit is its primary mission. An L3C can accept foundation funds in the form of program-related investments (PRIs), mission-related investments, loans, and guarantees (Hrywna 2009). B corporation is a designation that a for-profit corporation can seek to signal that they use the power of business to create public benefit (Certified B Corporation 2010; Environmental Leader 2009). The intent of the new for-profit designation is to make it easier for socially oriented businesses to attract program-related investments from foundations and additional money from private investors (Wallace 2009).

## Legal Challenges

Nonprofit agencies must comply with federal, state, and local laws, with executive orders, and with the rules and regulations promulgated by administrative agencies such as the Equal Employment Opportunity Commission, the Department of Labor, and the Internal Revenue Service, as well as with federal, state, and local government court decisions. Changes in tax rates have an impact on incentives for charitable contributions. The nonprofit community has expressed concern over President Obama's proposed tax changes. The tax break for donating a car to a charitable organization changed in 2004 and for donating works of art in 2006 (Dale 2008; Spector 2008), and there are federal and state laws that govern fund-raising and solicitation activities.

The Internal Revenue Service, in consultation with the National Association of State Charity Officials and Independent Sector, has developed a new Form 990 in an effort to improve the accountability and transparency of nonprofits.

It has been estimated that over 292,000 nonprofits may lose their tax-exempt status for failing to file a tax return with the IRS. The Pension Protection Act of 2006 requires that nonprofits (other than churches and church-related organizations) with gross receipts of less than $25,000 need to file the new Form 990-N, also known as the e-Postcard (Blackwood and Roeger 2010).

There was a recent attempt to suppress nonprofit advocacy efforts in the deliberation of the Edward M. Kennedy Serve America Act that was signed by President Obama on April 21, 2009. Nonprofit hospitals are facing scrutiny of the amount of charity care they are rendering, and some local governments are seeking to eliminate hospitals' property tax exemptions, along with those of other wealthy nonprofit institutions such as universities. Legislation has been introduced to the U.S. Senate to encourage foundations to give away more of their money (Strom 2009b), and the National Committee for Responsible Philanthropy (NCRP) continues to challenge foundations to spend more of their assets (Jagpal 2009). In New York, the state legislature recently adopted a budget plan that would limit the deduction that New York taxpayers who earn more than $10 million annually can claim on their state tax returns to only 25 percent of their charitable contributions rather than the current 50 percent (G. Williams 2010).

### Technological Challenges

Technology has changed the way many organizations operate. Grant applications are now often required to be submitted online. The recruitment of volunteers and staff is often done through the Internet, as are many fund-raising and advocacy activities. The Salvation Army has experimented with bell ringers' accepting debit and credit cards along with spare change, acknowledging that many consumers no longer carry cash. It also developed a pilot program to allow Ohioans to donate to the Red Kettle Campaigns by sending a text message to a number posted by the kettles. A five dollar donation will then be charged to their cell phone bills. Other Salvation Army divisions offer updates through Twitter, hoping to reach new people who do not donate through traditional appeals (Associated Press 2008; Franko 2008).

New York Philharmonic audience members attending a concert in Central Park voted for an encore through text messages, and other orchestras are experimenting as well. The Houston Symphony has a program called mSymphony, where people can sign up with a text message to receive special offers and alerts about weather for outdoor concerts or traffic problems near the traffic hall (Wakin 2010). Many nonprofits are holding webinars to reach their stakeholders, and social media are being used to a greater extent in fund-raising. However, not all nonprofits have the organizational capacity to be innovative. Many nonprofits are deficient in staff knowledge and skills and hardware and software capabilities. They may not have the financial resources to invest in the technology necessary to be more innovative. Some of the barriers to IT development include a lack of dedicated and flexible funding, inadequate time devoted to planning, not having a qualified IT staff person, capacities for using IT and understanding technology's role, and a lack of access to expertise and reliable information. As a result, nonprofits are perceived to be behind business and government in adopting technology (Manzo and Pitkin 2007).

### Social Challenges

The demographic composition of American society is changing. Hispanics (who can be of any race) are now the largest minority in the United States at approximately 48.4 million, 16 percent of the nation's population. As of 2008, the black or African American population, including those of more than one race, surpassed 41.1 million

(U.S. Census Bureau 2009), the Asian population was 19.9 million, American Indian and Alaskan Native 4.5 million, Native Hawaiian and other Pacific Islander 1 million. The number of Americans who declared themselves as two or more races is greater than 6 million. The population of non-Hispanic whites who indicated no other race totaled 198.7 million. The minority population in the United States is now at 100.7 million. Approximately one in three U.S. residents is a minority. Foreign-born workers make up approximately 15.3 percent of the civilian labor force sixteen years of age or older (ibid.). Nonprofit agencies need to evaluate whether or not their services and programs are meeting the needs of a changing community and, if not, make changes. Agencies need to make sure that they are not unlawfully discriminating against certain individuals in employment and volunteer opportunities. Americans who are sixty-five years and older constitute more than 38.9 million, 13 percent of the population. It is projected that in 2050, the population will increase to 88.5 million and will comprise 20 percent of the total population (U.S. Census Bureau 2010a).

Once the economy rebounds, agencies need to prepare for the impending retirements of traditionalists and baby boomers. They need to engage in workforce and succession planning, and develop strategies for sharing knowledge and experience. To survive in today's economy, nonprofit leaders, employees, and board members need to be comfortable moving in new directions and be ready for a greater emphasis on accountability.

## Conclusion

Nonprofit management must meet the challenge of declining revenues, changing social needs and priorities, and new directions in public policy, as well as pressures for increased accountability and productivity. To be effective, nonprofit administrators, board members, employees, and volunteers need to understand the context in which nonprofits operate. They need to increase their accountability to their various stakeholders, understand intergovernmental relations, and become more active in developing and implementing public policies, develop advocacy and financial management skills, recognize the human resources management challenges as well as opportunities facing them, and strive for improved organizational performance.

## Case 1.1. Selling Girl Scout Cookies by Internet

Eight-year-old Wild Freeborn from Asheville, North Carolina, starred in a YouTube video in which she bounced around a couch and encouraged viewers with the sales pitch "Buy cookies! And they're yummy!" An online order form and promotional material were posted along with the video. Girl Scouts of the USA forbids Internet cookie sales. One reason is the dangers young girls can encounter on the Web, and there is also the issue of fairness. Local councils typically award prizes to girls for reaching certain levels of sales, and since girls are limited to selling within their local areas, a campaign can overwhelm opportunities for girls in other towns. Wild's father says that although his daughter took orders online, she delivered the cookies and collected payment in person. "Wild did everything you do as a traditional cookie-selling Girl Scout, but she also utilized the Internet to promote the cookies." Mr. Freeborn, a guest lecturer at the University of North Carolina at Asheville, assigned his mass communications class to run a "grassroots" cookie campaign on his daughter's behalf, using Facebook, Craigslist, and text messaging, directed at Asheville residents.

The local council received complaints from parents of other scouts about Wild's campaign, so the online order form was removed but kept up a video, a Facebook page, and a PayPal account through which people could donate cookies to charities or the military.

The chief executive of the local organization, Girl Scouts of Western North Carolina–Pisgah Council, agreed that Wild's approach violated national regulations, but stated, "It's a new day now—to not develop a system for girls to sell via the Internet is probably not responding to how girls operate these days. But as long as there's a rule, we need to support it or at least enforce it, not to defy the rule or misinterpret the rule." The national spokesman for the Girl Scouts of the USA says that rule may change. "We need to find a way to come up with a program for girls to sell cookies that is safe and fair; once we do we will allow online sales."

*Source:* Brown 2009.

## Case 1.2. Centro Latino de Chelsea and
## Concilio Hispano to Merge

Due to the troubled economy amidst a growing demand for services, two small nonprofits that serve primarily Latino and immigrant communities north of Boston merged to provide health, educational, and workforce training services. Centro Latino de Chelsea and Concilio Hispano in Cambridge will form Centro Latino, Inc., based in Chelsea. The new organization will have a budget of $2.2 million and expects to serve more than 7,000 people in at least two dozen cities and neighborhoods. The organizations have partnered in the past and began talking about joining forces last year. Centro Latino de Chelsea was looking to expand but did not because of funding cutbacks caused by the recession, and Concilio Hispano needed a leader. It had been without an executive director for approximately two years.

The chief executive of Centro Latino notes, "We've got the economy, we've got this huge growth of Latinos and immigrants in general. It only gets you so far, being a smaller organization with the pressure from the economy and the demand growing so dramatically. We said we have to do this better, we have got to do this more efficiently."

The director of consulting services at the Nonprofit Finance Fund that helped with the merger stated, "Together, what they are going to be able to do is position themselves to serve the Latino community in a much better way in the future than they would have been able to do alone." The president of The Boston Foundation, a philanthropic nonprofit, said agencies like his as well as others that provide funds to nonprofits have a responsibility to encourage such collaborations. "There's no question that a lot of mature organizations have overlapping missions."

*Source:* Ailworth 2009.

## References

Ailworth, E. (2009). Nonprofit immigrant-aid groups to merge. *Boston Globe*, April 1. www.boston.com/business/articles/2009/04/01/nonprofit_immigrant_aid_groups_to_merge/.

Anderson, Z. (2010). Nonprofits worry that growth is fleeting. *Sarasota Herald Tribune*, April 21, BN1. www.heraldtribune.com/article/20100421/ARTICLE/4211036.

Associated Press (2008). No change? Swipe your card at a kettle. *New York Times*, November 14(219).

Azam, M.S. (2009). United Way alters funding approach. *Orlando Business Journal*, April 3. www.bizjournals.com/orlando/stories/2009/04/06/story1.html?page=2.

Banjo, S. (2009). Next benefit to face the ax: Matching gifts. *Wall Street Journal.* January 14. http://online.wsj.com/article/SB123188973119079037.html.

Blackwood, A., and K.L. Roeger (2010). Here today, gone tomorrow: A look at organizations that may have their tax-exempt status revoked. Report, July 8. Washington, DC: Urban Institute.

Bosman, J. (2009). Newly poor swell lines at food banks. *New York Times*, February 20, A1.

Brown, R. (2009). Girl Scouts battle with one of their own. *New York Times*, March 19, A17.

Certified B Corporation (2010). www.bcorporation.net.

Chen, D.W. (2010). At least 50 of the city's senior centers expected to close to save money. *New York Times*, April 30, A15.

Connolly, C. (2009). In North Carolina, recession breeds a health-care crisis. *Washington Post*, April 20. www.washingtonpost.com/wp-dyn/content/article/2009/04/19/AR2009041902239.html.

Couloumbis, A. (2010). Rendell warns of Pennsylvania job losses without aid from Congress. Philly.com, August 4. www.philly.com/philly/news/politics/state/20100804_Rendell_warns_of_Pennsylvania_job_losses_without_aid_from_Congress.html.

Dale, A. (2008). Tax breaks for donating a car. *Wall Street Journal,* July 25. http://online.wsj.com/article/SB121700900414785291.html.

Douglas, J. (1983). *Why charity? The case for the third sector.* Beverly Hills, CA: Sage.

Eckholm, E. (2009). States slashing social programs for vulnerable. *New York Times*, April 12. www.nytimes.com/2009/04/12/us/12deficit.html.

Environmental Leader (2009). B corporations gain tax advantage in Philly. December 4. www.environmentalleader.com/2009/12/04/b-corporations-gain-tax-advantage-in-philly/.

Fountain, H. (2009). In zoo cuts, it's man vs. beast. *New York Times*, March 19, F28.

Franko, K. (2008). Salvation Army tries text donations in Ohio. Associated Press, October 22. In Philly.com, www.philly.com/philly/wires/ap/features/high_teach/20081022_ap_salvationarmytriestextdonationsinohio.html?adString=ph.wires/high_teach;!category=high_tech;&randomOrd=102308112022.

Giving USA (2010). Giving USA 2010: The annual report on philanthropy for the year 2009. Giving Foundation USA. www.givingusa.org.

Glader, P. (2008). GE foundation switches donation focus to basic needs. *Wall Street Journal*, December 19.

Goldstein, A. (2009). More need, less help. As South Carolina's job losses mount, agencies and charities stymied by budget cuts and politics. *Washington Post*, March 12, A01.

Greenwell, M., and H. R. Harris (2009). Four area boys and girls clubs to close. *Washington Post*, April 9, B01.

Healy, P. (2009). Nonprofit theatres say next season may be their toughest yet. *New York Times*, April 4. www.nytimes.com/2009/04/04/theater/04offb.html.

Hrywna, M. (2009). The L3C status: Groups explore structure that limits liability for program-related investing. *Nonprofit Times*, 23 (17), 1, 8.

Husch, B., M. Barton, L. Cummings, S. Mazer, and B. Stigritz (2010). *The fiscal survey of the states: June 2010*. Washington, DC: National Association of State Budget Officers. www.nasbo.org.

Internal Revenue Service (IRS) (2010). Publication 557: Tax-exempt status for your organization. www.irs.gov/pub/irs-pdf/p557.pdf.

Jagpal, N. (2009). Criteria for philanthropy at its best: Benchmarks to assess and enhance grantmaker impact. www.ncrp.org/files/publications/paib-fulldoc_lowres.pdf.

Kostrze, J. (2008). Nonprofit groups turn to survival strategies. *Providence Journal*, September 7. www.projo.com/business/content/BZ_JK0907_09–07–08_HPBF66I_v14.4003c6.html.

Lampman, J. (2009). Economic downturn frays America's safety net. *Christian Science Monitor*, January 26. www.csmonitor.com/Business/2009/0126/p10s01-usec.html.

Manzo, P., and B. Pitkin (2007). Barriers to information technology usage in the nonprofit sector. In *Nonprofits and technology: Emerging research for usable knowledge*, ed. M. Cortés and K.M. Rafter, 51–67. Chicago: Lyceum Books.

McGill, L.T., and S. Lawrence. (2009) Grantmakers describe the impact of the economic crisis on their giving. Foundation Center Research Series, March. http://foundationcenter.org/gainknowledge/research/econ_outlook4.html.

National Center for Charitable Statistics (NCCS) (2010). Number of nonprofit organizations in the United States, 1998–2008. http://nccsdataweb.urban.org/PubApps/profile1.php?state=US. Retrieved 1/27/2010.

National Council of Nonprofits (2010). State budget crises: Ripping the safety net held by nonprofits. March 16. Washington, DC: www.councilofnonprofits.org.

Nonprofit Finance Fund (2009). Nonprofit Finance Fund survey: America's nonprofits in danger. April 19. www.nonprofitfinancefund.org.

Oleck, H.L. (1988). Nonprofit corporations, organizations, and associations (5th ed.). Upper Saddle River, NJ: Prentice Hall.

O'Neill, M. (1989). The third America: The emergence of the nonprofit sector in the United States. San Francisco: Jossey-Bass.

Pogrebin, R. (2009). New York's local museums feel the pinch. *New York Times*, March 19, SPG6.

Prah, P.M. (2009). State budget gaps top $200 billion; fees, tax hikes in the works. *Stateline*, April 24. www.stateline.org/live/details/story?contentId=394944.

Press of Atlantic City Staff (2010). Legal services nonprofit to lay off a third of its staff due to cuts in state funding. PressofAtlanticCity.com, August 2. www.pressofatlanticcity.com/news/breaking/article_b33d5cf0–9e74–11df-91aa-001cc4c002e0.html.

Rathburn, A. (2010). Monroe considers cutting staff, YMCA pledge to fill budget hole. *Daily Herald*, July 29. www.heraldnet.com/article/20100729/NEWS01/707299788.

Royce, G. (2009). Walker trims budget by $2 million this year, next. *Star Tribune*, March 17. www.startribune.com/entertainment/art/41334892.html.

Salamon, L.M. (1999). *America's nonprofit sector: A primer.* (2nd ed.). New York: Foundation Center.

———. 2002). The resilient sector: The state of nonprofit America. In *The state of nonprofit America*, ed. Lester M. Salamon, 9–11. Washington, DC: Brookings Institution Press.

Sataline, S. (2008). In hard times, houses of God turn to chapter 11 in book of bankruptcy. *Wall Street Journal*, December 23. http://online.wsj.com/article/SB122999261138328613.html.

Sheets, H.M. (2009). Taking a step-by-step approach to growth. *New York Times*, March 19, SPG 2.

Spector, M. (2008). A portrait of art as a tax deduction. *Wall Street Journal*, July 22, D1.

Stobbe, M. (2009). Public health centers struggle to keep up. Boston.com., March 13. www.boston.com/news/nation/articles/2009/03/13/public_health_centers_struggle_to_keep_up/.

Strom, S. (2008). Wall St. fraud leaves charities reeling. *New York Times*, December 16. www.nytimes.com/2008/12/16/business/16charity.html.

————. (2009a). Charities now seek bankruptcy protection. *New York Times*, February 20, A17.

————. (2009b). Senate measure seeks to spur foundations to give more. *New York Times*, March 25, A20.

————. (2009c). Foundation giving in '08 defied huge assets decline. *New York Times*, March 31, A16.

U.S. Census Bureau (2009). Black (African-American) Month: February 2009. U.S. Census Bureau News, CB10-FF.01.

————. (2010a). Older Americans Month: May 2010. U.S. Census Bureau News, CB10-FF.06.

————. (2010b). Hispanic Heritage Month 2010: Sept. 15–Oct. 15. U.S. Census Bureau News, CB10–FF.17.

Vestal, C. (2009). States cope with rising homelessness. *Stateline*, March 18. www.stateline.org/live/details/story?contentId=385137.

Wakin, D.J. (2010). Orchestras seek BFF by cell phone texts. *New York Times*, July 21, C1.

Wallace, N. (2009). New legal status for socially oriented business gains ground. *Chronicle of Philanthropy*, April 15. http://philanthropy.com/blogs/conference/new-legal-status-for-socially-oriented-business-gains-ground/10514.

Weisbrod, B.A. (1997). The future of the nonprofit sector: It's entwining with private enterprise and government. *Journal of Policy Analysis and Management*, 16 (4), 541–555.

Weitzman, M.S., N.T. Jalandoni, L.M. Lampkin, and T.H. Pollak (2002). *The new nonprofit almanac and desk reference: The essential facts and figures for managers, researchers, and volunteers.* San Francisco: Jossey-Bass.

White, G., C. Quinn, A. Miller, P. Ruhe, R. Grantham, L. Diamond, and T. Joyner (2009). The state of nonprofits: Gifts don't meet demands. *Atlanta Journal-Constitution*, February 1. www.ajc.com/hotjobs/content/printedition/2009/02/01/charity02013dot.html.

Williams, G. (2010). New York legislature passes plan to limit charitable deductions for the wealthy. *Chronicle of Philanthropy*, August 4. http://philanthropy.com/article/New-York-Legislature-Passes/123757/.

Williams, L.C. (2010). 11 Seattle homeless shelters may close soon. *Seattle Times*, August 3. http://seattletimes.nwsource.com/html/localnews/2012516720_homeless03m.html.

# ————— 2 —————

# Increased Accountability in the Nonprofit Sector

It is almost impossible to read a newspaper or turn on the news without hearing about dishonest behavior by nonprofit agencies and the lack of oversight by nonprofit boards of directors. Nonprofit hospitals have come under scrutiny about how much free care they provide to the poor, patient billing practices, and their relationship with for-profit organizations. Legislation being considered in the U.S. Senate would require hospitals to spend a minimum amount on free care to indigent individuals and set curbs on executive compensation and conflicts of interest (Carreyrou and Martinez 2008; Shrives 2010).

The salaries and perks of nonprofit executive directors have also come under scrutiny. The former chief executive of the Smithsonian Institution, Lawrence M. Small, was reimbursed nearly $90,000 in expenses without submitting documentation, in violation of the Smithsonian Institution's policies. Other questionable expenses include chartering a Lear jet and first-class airfare, and a $197,322 housing allowance that included "mortgage interest" payments on a 8.3 percent loan, even though Mr. Small did not have a mortgage and the average rate of a mortgage at that time was 5.9 percent. Mr. Small's compensation grew to almost $916,000 in 2007. He resigned in March 2007 when it was also revealed that he charged the Smithsonian Institution for housekeeping, repairs to his home swimming pool, and other expenses. The organization Citizens for Responsibility and Ethics in Washington asked the U.S. attorney general to investigate whether Small broke the law by using federal money to pay for some of his personal expenses. It also asked the Justice Department to look into whether the Smithsonian's board broke the law by approving the expenses. Since then, the Smithsonian Institution, which includes the National Zoo and the National Air and Space Museum, has commissioned independent reviews of its governance and compensation policies, established a code of ethics, and made changes to its board structure (Grimaldi 2007; Grimaldi and Trescott 2007a, 2007b, 2008; Olson 2007a, 2007b; Trescott 2008; Zongker 2007, 2008).

Some local United Way agencies have double-counted donations, considered the value of volunteers' time as contributions, and taken credit for contributions that were handled or raised for competing organizations in shared campaigns as a way to make their contributions greater and their expenses smaller (Salmon 2006; Strom 2002a, 2002b).

The United Way of Central Carolinas spent hundreds of thousands of dollars in salaries to operate four in-house programs run by agency staff while counting it as charitable activity instead of overhead. That allowed the United Way to appear to be sending a larger share of its donations to community agencies than it actually did. This is the same United Way that was criticized for paying its president $1.2 million in compensation in 2007 (Hall and Frazier 2008). And more recently, the board of directors at United Way of Tucson and Southern Arizona decided not to release reports from two auditing firms hired to find out why it lost track of its cash flow and fell behind in payments to local charities (Alaimo 2010).

A report by the Government Accountability Office (GAO) found that nearly 55,000 exempt organizations had almost $1 billion in unpaid federal taxes as of September 30, 2006. About 1,500 of these entities each had over $100,000 in federal tax debts, with some owing tens of millions of dollars (GAO 2007).

Other well-publicized lapses can be found much earlier (Gibelman and Gelman 2001; Gibelman et al.1997; Greenlee et al. 2007; Herzlinger 1996). The United Way of America scandal with William Aramony in the 1990s called attention to lax oversight by boards of directors and what was perceived to be overly generous compensation for an executive of a nonprofit organization. The American Red Cross came under fire for fund-raising tactics after September 11, 2001, as well as for its financial reporting practices and disaster relief policies. The Nature Conservancy has been scrutinized as a result of its governance, sweetheart land transactions with board members, and management practices. As noted earlier, concerns about financial improprieties and the management of donations in a number of local United Way organizations required that the United Way of America adopt new rules for local affiliates to disclose more information to the public and meet new financial accounting standards (Ottaway and Stephens 2003; Stamler

2004; Stephens and Ottaway 2003a, 2003b, 2003c, 2005). Senators Tom Coburn (R-Oklahoma), John Corny (R-Texas), Charles Grassley (R-Iowa), and Jon Kyl (R-Arizona) have recently asked Boys & Girls Clubs of America to provide more information about what it spends on executive compensation, lobbying, perks, travel, and other items. They are troubled by some of the group's expenses at the time it reported a $13 million loss on its 2008 tax return. Its president earned more than $900,000 in compensation; more than $4 million was spent on travel, $1.6 million on conferences, and more than $540,000 on lobbying. This is while local Boys & Girls Clubs were closing due to budget reductions (Kinzie 2010; Perry 2008).

These examples are just a snapshot of what is happening across the country and in many of our own communities. A lack of accountability can be found in many (not all) nonprofits, large and small. Nonprofits are expected to be accountable in their governance, finances, performance, and fidelity to their mission (Ebrahim 2010).

This chapter will provide a brief overview of the importance of accountability in the nonprofit sector, posing the following questions:

1. Why has the ethical behavior of nonprofit administrators and boards of directors come under greater scrutiny?
2. What are the management benefits and challenges for the increased emphasis on nonprofit accountability?
3. What management skills and leader behaviors are necessary for ethical practices?

The excessive salaries and perks paid to some nonprofit executives and foundation trustees, the self-dealing of many philanthropies, the failure to meet their public service commitment, the lack of oversight provided by many nonprofit boards of directors, foundations not investing in urban communities or rural areas, as well as spending little money beyond the 5 percent required by law have all been contributing factors in the demand for greater oversight, transparency, and accountability of 501(c)(3) nonprofits. David R. Jones, president and chief executive officer of the Community Service Society (CSS) of New York and board chair of the National Committee for Responsible Philanthropy (NCRP), made the following statement when asked in an interview, "What is the primary issue in the philanthropic sector you are most concerned about?"

My foremost concern in the field of philanthropy—and I have been pretty public about it—is the lack of accountability. I have worked in the private sector—I was a corporate lawyer for some years; I have worked in government; and I have been the chair of a for-profit institution. I have never seen a sector that has less ability for external forces to really motivate it to change. I think this sector needs to be brought under some political pressure. There is no accountability to the public despite the fact we are using the tax code and public resources to underwrite these grantmaking institutions. If the situation does not change, I think it is going to continue to go off the rails. Everything these institutions do has to be subjected to overt public scrutiny and not some secret process. (NCRP 2007, 9)

While recent transgressions in the nonprofit sector have garnered media attention, concerns about the management of nonprofit organizations and foundations extends back to 1961 when Representative Wright Patman (D-Texas), chairman of the House Subcommittee on Small Business and the House Banking and Currency Committee, launched congressional investigations into the alleged financial abuses by foundations (Billitteri 2000; Subcommittee Chairman's Report to Subcommittee No. 1, Select Committee on Small Business 1962–1972; U.S. Senate Committee on Finance 1965). The Tax Reform Act of 1969 imposed strict rules to prevent donors or their relatives or associates from using foundations for private gain and required foundations to distribute a minimum amount of their assets each year for charitable purposes. Foundations were also required to pay an annual excise tax on investment income, curb their lobbying activities, diversify their stock holdings, and exercise prudent investment standards when investing assets. The act imposed stricter disclosure rules on foundations than on charities. The Commission on Private Philanthropy and Public Needs was created in 1973 by John D. Rockefeller III, who asked insurance executive John Filer to chair the commission, which became known as the "Filer Commission." The Filer Commission investigated the scope and impact of the work done by foundations and charities and their relationships with business and government. In 1974, state attorney generals formed a new coalition to coordinate the enforcement of charity laws across the states. There was a concern that many groups were neglected by established philanthropy, which led to the creation of the National Committee for Responsive Philanthropy in 1976. In 1983 the U.S. Supreme Court ruled that nonprofits are not entitled to tax-exempt status if they operate "contrary to established public policy and are at odds with the common community conscience." In 1987, the IRS required nonprofits to show their Form 990 information to anyone who made a request in person. More recently, in 1996, Congress passed a law that enabled the IRS to penalize charity officials who received or approved inappropriately high compensation. The law also required nonprofits to make their Form 990 informational tax returns easily accessible to the public (Billitteri 2000, 29–32).

The corporate scandals involving Enron, WorldCom, Fannie Mae, HealthSouth, Bank of America, Citigroup, Goldman Sachs, Ernst & Young, JPMorgan, Bank One, Strong Capital Management, Putnam Investments, Prudential Securities, Arthur Andersen, Deloitte & Touche, Global Crossing, Kellogg, Brown & Root, Merrill Lynch, Qwest, AIG, and Tyco International helped to facilitate the passage of the Public Company Accounting Reform and Investor Protection Act in 2002, more commonly known as the Sarbanes-Oxley Act, named after Senator Paul Sarbanes (D-Maryland) and Representative Michael Oxley (R-Ohio), who were its main sponsors. The act was passed to restore public trust in the corporate community in the wake of the corporate and accounting scandals, by requiring publicly traded companies to conform to standards in governance, financial transactions, and audit procedures. Two provisions in the law pertained to nonprofits, strengthened whistleblower protection, and the retention of documents related to lawsuits. In 2003 and 2006, Independent Sector and Board Source published *Learning from Sarbanes-Oxley: A Checklist for Nonprofits and Foundations*. An abbreviated checklist can be found in Appendix 2.1.

## Federal and State Oversight of Nonprofit Organizations

Several government agencies are charged with monitoring and regulating charitable organizations. Most states have their own laws governing the creation, operation, and dissolution of charitable organizations. In most states, attorneys general bear the primary responsibility for enforcing these laws and investigating complaints of fraud or abuse of tax-exempt status. State charity regulators monitor adherence to charitable solicitations laws, investigate complaints of fraud or abuse of tax-exempt status, and maintain lists of registered nonprofit organizations.

At the federal level, the IRS's Division on Tax Exempt and Government Entities reviews applications for tax-exempt status, audits a sample of Form 990s filed annually by nonprofits, and enforces the requirements imposed by the tax code on charitable organizations. The IRS is also authorized to assess fines and penalties and, as a last resort, to revoke tax-exempt status.

However, a serious shortage of resources has often made it difficult to identify and punish most violators. While the number of charitable organizations has more than doubled since 1974, the staffing of the IRS-exempt organizations division has increased only incrementally.

In 2004, Senator Charles Grassley (R-Iowa), chairman of the Senate Finance Committee, and Senator Max Baucus (D-Montana) sent a letter to the Independent Sector encouraging it to convene an independent group of leaders from the charitable sector to consider and recommend actions to strengthen the governance, ethical conduct, and accountability within public charities and private foundations. The result was the following report from the Panel on the Nonprofit Sector: *Strengthening the Transparency, Governance, and Accountability of Charitable Organizations: A Final Report to Congress and the Nonprofit Sector* (2005). A follow-up report titled *Strengthening the Transparency, Governance, and Accountability of Charitable Organizations: A Supplement to the Final Report to Congress and the Nonprofit Sector* was issued in April 2006, and *Principles for Good Governance and Ethical Practice: A Guide for Charities and Foundations* was issued in October 2007. A summary of the recommendations from the reports can be found in Appendices 2.2 and 2.3.

### Revisions to IRS Form 990 for Charitable Institutions

Nonprofits with gross annual receipts of 25,000 or higher are required to submit a completed IRS Form 990 to the Internal Revenue Service (IRS). Until this past year, Form 990 had not been revised since 1979. The IRS recognized that Form 990 failed to keep pace with the increasing size, diversity, and complexity of the tax-exempt sector, and that it failed to meet tax-compliance issues and the transparency and accountability needs of state governments, the general public, and the local communities served by nonprofits. Smaller tax-exempt nonprofits with annual gross receipts below $25,000 did not have to file Form 990s annually, but now every year must file a new form titled "Electronic Notice (e-Postcard) for Tax-Exempt Organizations Not Required to File Form 990 or 990-EZ." Requiring small nonprofits to file annually with the IRS will provide a more complete count of nonprofits than currently exists.

The National Association of State Charity Officials (NASCO) worked with the IRS to develop the new form. Its summary page gives a snapshot of the nonprofit's key financial, governance, and operating information, and then a description of the organization's program service accomplishments to provide context before the examiner proceeds to sections on tax compliance, governance, compensation, and financial statements. There is now a checklist of required supplemental schedules that give a quick view of whether the nonprofit is conducting activities the IRS would be concerned about. The Checklist of Required Schedules also provides a quick view of whether the filing nonprofit is conducting activities that raise tax-compliance concerns, such as lobbying or political campaign activities, transactions with interested persons, transactions with insiders or family members or closely associated businesses and major dispositions of assets. It also indicates which schedules the nonprofit is required to file with the form.

The revised Form 990 requires the nonprofit to describe the composition of its board or governing body, its governance policies and practices, and the means by which it is held accountable to the public by making governance and financial information publicly available. It is believed that nonprofits that are well managed and have knowledgeable oversight are more likely to be transparent with regard to their operations, their finances, their fund-raising practices, and the use of their assets for exempt purposes.

Also provided will be a summary of the nonprofit's financial activity comparing the current and prior years' revenues, expenses, assets, and liabilities. The nonprofit is required to list its mission or most significant activities, the number of independent and nonindependent directors, and the number of employees and volunteers. The amount of the nonprofit's unrelated business income and unrelated business taxable income will also be included.

Nonprofits are required to describe their tax-exempt-purpose achievements for their three largest programs, the resources spent on each of the programs in the prior year, and whether the nonprofit discontinued any core programs since the last filing. The Statement of Functional Expenses illustrates how much of every dollar nonprofits spend on non-program activities such as fund-raising and management.

Form 990 asks for additional information in regard to governance, management, and disclosure, names of those on the board of directors, the number of board members eligible to vote, the number of independent members, and any family or business relationships among board members, their families, or the organization's employees and vendors. Nonprofits must also identify their organizations' board structure, policies, and practices.

Additional information now required to be part of the IRS review include whether nonprofits have conflict-of-interest policies, whether completed Form 990s are posted on their websites, and whether there was an annual compensation review by independent persons using comparable data and other factors.

There is also an expanded review of key employees, officers, directors, and contractor compensation. Full compensation must be disclosed for all key employees and current board members. Nonprofits must disclose their five highest-paid employees and independent contractors making more than $100,000 per year, and whether former board members or key employees were paid more than $100,000 in the prior year. Included in Form 990 is the requirement that nonprofits describe the process for determining the compensation of the CEO, executive director, other officers, and key employees.

The IRS believes that it is important to determine if the organization has safeguards in place to make sure its assets are protected and will be used for exempt purposes. These considerations are even more important for nonprofits subject to the prohibitions on private benefit, excess benefit, and private inurement.

## Types of Accountability

Sound financial management is not the only type of accountability that nonprofits need to be concerned with. They must also be attentive to fairness and performance. *Fairness accountability* addresses the expectation of having services and procedures apply to people equitably. Fair decisions are made according to impartial standards rather than being based on favoritism. *Performance accountability* refers to how service activities are implemented, how successful the activities are, and whether desired outcomes result. And *financial accountability* is the expectation that funds will be administered in an honest and responsible manner, commonly in accordance with generally accepted accounting practices (Whitaker et al. 2003).

## Nonprofit Ethics

In addition to external formal controls such as federal, state, and local government tax-compliance forms, government and foundation program reports and audits, and financial audits prepared by public accounting firms, it is important that nonprofits establish an internal ethical climate. Professional organizations routinely promote ethical behavior among their members through the creation and promulgation of codes of ethics, but the promotion of ethical behavior is not sufficient. Denhardt (1988, 1) notes that "managing ethics involves more than making public statements espousing a particular set of values and more than selecting employees with good moral character. Managing ethics also involves careful analysis of the organizational culture, working to develop a cultural environment that enables organizational members to act with ethical integrity."

In the introduction of a special edition of *Academy of Management Executive*, titled "Ethical Behavior in Management: Bringing Ethics into the Mainstream," the guest editor notes, "Now more than ever, managerial ethics are being called into question. While it is almost a cliché to make such a statement, the fact is that management scholars have not sufficiently addressed ethics within mainstream research agendas" (Veiga 2004, 37). Despite disappointing corporate performance, more than 500 corporate fraud convictions, the need to reissue financial reports, dishonest research reports, and inflated stock prices, CEO compensation has increased. The attention that was focused on CEO behavior has not brought about long-lasting changes in corporate boardrooms (Deutsch 2005; Eichenwald 2005; Johnson 2005).

While business colleges have begun to address the importance of ethics training in their undergraduate and graduate curriculums, public administration has been concerned with ethics since the 1920s. The International City County Managers Association (ICMA) developed the *ICMA Code of Ethics* in 1924 and has revised it over the years. The American Society of Public Administration (ASPA) developed a *Set of Moral Principles* in 1981 and a *Code of Ethics* in 1984, and, like ICMA, makes periodic revisions to keep them relevant. Likewise, the National Association of Social Workers (NASW) approved the *NASW Code of Ethics* in 1996 and revised it in 2008. Other professions have codes of ethics as well.

Independent Sector (IS), a coalition of corporate giving programs, foundations, and private voluntary organizations formed to support nonprofits, believes that each and every organization in the independent sector should have a code of ethics. IS firmly believes that the process by which a code is adopted is as important as the code itself, and that the board and staff should be involved in developing, drafting, adopting, and implementing a statement that fits the organization's unique characteristics.

> We encourage all organizations to set aside time in your board meeting or at a retreat to discuss in detail all aspects of an ethical code—and be sure that new board members have the appropriate orientation to understand and embrace your code of ethics and practices.

Any code of ethics is built on a foundation of widely shared values. Independent Sector's values include the following:

- Commitment of the public good
- Accountability to the public
- Commitment beyond the law
- Respect for the worth and dignity of individuals
- Inclusiveness and social justice
- Respect for pluralism and diversity
- Transparency, integrity, and honesty
- Responsible stewardship of resources
- Commitment to excellence and to maintaining the public trust (Independent Sector, 2010)

The values inform and guide the actions that organizations should take in developing their policies and practices.

## Whistle-Blower Protection

A whistle-blower is an employee, former employee, or contractor of an agency who reports agency misconduct. Generally, the misconduct is a violation of law, rule, or regulation or a direct threat to public interest, such as fraud, health/safety violations, or corruption. The whistle-blower laws and policies are designed to protect employees against retaliation for reporting wrongdoing, illegal conduct, internal fraud, and discrimination (Harshbarger and Crafts 2007). The federal government and many states and local governments have some sort of statutory or common law "whistle-blower" or anti-retaliation laws. Many nonprofits have developed their own internal whistle-blower policies as well. Harshbarger and Crafts (2007) note that internal whistle-blower policies can be used to identify problems in the workplace.

With whistle-blower protections in place, intervention and prevention methods can strengthen and support a workplace culture of integrity, openness, transparency, and two-way communication (p. 38). Even without internal policies, nonprofits have been advised to adhere to the whistle-blowing provisions of the Sarbanes-Oxley Act. Public and nonprofit employers need to be aware of the Whistle Blower Protection Act of 1989, the state and local laws in jurisdictions in which they are located, as well as comply with any internal policies that have been adopted in regard to whistle-blowers.

## Conclusion

Many public charities and foundations have been remiss in meeting their obligations to the public good. This has resulted in less confidence in the sector and demands for greater oversight (Perry 2008). Nonprofits have been found to inflate membership numbers, double-count donations, and not meet their public purpose in delivering services. Chief executives and board members (or trustees) have benefited from self-dealing. In other instances, the boards were negligent in exercising their fiduciary and oversight responsibilities. Members of Congress, the IRS, and state attorneys general are investigating if nonprofits are awarding their leaders too much in salary and other forms of compensation, including loans and deferred payments—behaviors that had become common in for-profit organizations (Stamler 2004). To regain the confidence of the community, the U.S. Congress, state attorneys general, donors, funders, and individuals, nonprofits need to commit to behaving in a lawful and ethical manner.

BBB Wise Giving Alliance (2003, 2010) has recently released a list of its standards that national charities commonly fail to meet when evaluated against its *Standards for Charity Accountability*. The most frequent violations include:

- Not having an annual report available on request that includes recommended programs, governance, and financial disclosures;
- Not having a policy of assessing within two years the nonprofit's performance and effectiveness and then determining the future actions required to meet its mission;
- Not submitting to the board for its approval a written report that outlines the results of the performance and effectiveness assessment and recommendations for future action;

- Not having a minimum of three meetings per year of the complete governing board with a majority in attendance;
- Not including on the nonprofit's website that solicits contributions the same information that is required for annual reports, as well as the mailing address of the nonprofit and electronic access to its most recent IRS Form 990.

---

### Case 2.1. Allegations of Steering Clients in a Homebuyer Education Program to an Affiliated Mortgage Company

It has been alleged that the Housing and Education Alliance, a nonprofit agency that helps prepare low-income residents to buy their first house, has steered clients to an affiliated mortgage company owned by the director or at times, the director's fiancé, of the nonprofit. The class covers making a budget to choosing a mortgage broker to knowing what is expected at the closing. It is suppose to keep residents from being taken advantage of. Many of the clients taught by the alliance are paying more than expected because of a yield-spread premium fee tacked on by their mortgage broker. A yield-spread premium is a fee paid to mortgage brokers for their services. The broker receives the money outside of closing from the bank funding the loan. It essentially increases the interest rate for the life of the loan, in exchange for a reduced out-of-pocket cost to the buyer at closing. Not all of the clients were told that a yield-spread premium would be attached to the loans. The agency has signed a contract with the county government to teach education classes for two years, but cancelled the contract when the county asked to include a conflict-of-interest clause that would have blocked the agency and the mortgage company from mutually benefiting from affordable housing clients.

Later in the year, the mortgage company said it would no longer work with the county's affordable housing program after housing officials banned mortgage brokers from receiving yield-spread premiums, which raises the interest rate on loans and forces home buyers to pay more for their homes than expected.

*Sources:* Allman 2008 and 2009.

## Case 2.2. Do Nonprofit Hospitals Earn Their Tax Breaks?

Members of Congress have raised concerns over whether nonprofit hospitals provide enough free care and other community benefits to justify their tax exemptions. There is, however, no test for measuring how much community benefit is enough or even what constitutes community benefit. One hospital benefit may be producing pamphlets on the importance of prenatal care, while another may be the cost of treating uninsured patients.

The Internal Revenue Service released a study indicating that nonprofit hospitals vary in the amount and type of charitable benefits they provide to the communities they serve. The almost 500 hospitals responding to the IRS survey reported spending an average of 9 percent of their total revenues on providing community benefits, including free medical care, education, and research.

An additional finding of the study was that most hospitals followed proper procedures in establishing salaries and benefits for their executives.

*Sources:* Strom 2009; IRS 2009.

## APPENDIX 2.1.
## LEARNING FROM SARBANES-OXLEY:
## A CHECKLIST FOR NONPROFITS AND FOUNDATIONS

1.  Insider Transactions and Conflicts of Interest
    *   Understand and fully comply with all laws regarding compensation and benefits provided to directors and executives (including "intermediate sanctions" and "self-dealing" laws).
    *   Do not provide personal loans to directors and executives.
    *   In cases in which the board feels it is necessary to provide a loan, however, all terms should be disclosed and formally approved by the board, the process should be documented, and the terms and the value of the loan should be publicly disclosed.
    *   Establish a conflict-of-interest policy and a regular and rigorous means of enforcing it.

2. Independent and Competent Audit Committee
   - Conduct an annual external financial audit (the boards of very small organizations, for which the cost of an external audit may be too burdensome, should at least evaluate carefully whether an audit would be valuable).
   - Establish a separate audit committee of the board.
   - Board members on the audit committee should be free from conflicts of interest and should not receive any compensation for their service on the committee.
   - Include at least one "financial expert" on the audit committee.
   - The audit committee should select and oversee the auditing company and review the audit.
   - Require full board to approve audit results.
   - Provide financial literacy training to all board members.
3. Responsibilities of Auditors
   - Rotate auditor or lead partner at least every five years.
   - Avoid any conflict of interest in staff exchange between audit firm and organization.
   - Do not use auditing firm for non-auditing services except tax form preparation with pre-approval from audit committee.
   - Require disclosure to audit committee of critical accounting policies and practices.
   - Use audit committee to oversee and enforce conflict-of-interest policy.
4. Certified Financial Statements
   - CEO and CFO should sign off on all financial statements (either formally or in practice), including Form 990 tax returns, to ensure they are accurate, complete, and filed on time.
   - The board should review and approve financial statements and Form 990 tax returns for completeness and accuracy.
5. Disclosure
   - Disclose Form 990 and 990-PF in a current and easily accessible way (also required of all nonprofit organizations by IRS law).
   - File Forms 990 and 990-PF in a timely manner, without use of extensions unless required by unusual circumstances.
   - Disclose audited financial statements.
   - Move to electronic filing of Forms 990 and 990-PF.

6. Whistle-Blower Protection
   - Develop, adopt, and disclose a formal process to deal with complaints and prevent retaliation.
   - Investigate employee complaints and correct any problems or explain why corrections are not necessary.
7. Document Destruction
   - Have a written, mandatory document retention and periodic destruction policy, which includes guidelines for electronic files and voice mail.
   - If an official investigation is under way or even suspected, stop any document-purging in order to avoid criminal obstruction (Independent Sector 2003).

---

## APPENDIX 2.2.
## PRINCIPLES FOR GOOD GOVERNANCE AND ETHICAL PRACTICE: A GUIDE FOR CHARITIES AND FOUNDATIONS

### Legal Compliance and Public Disclosure

1. A charitable organization must comply with all applicable federal laws and regulations, as well as applicable laws and regulations of the states and the local jurisdictions in which it is based or operates. If the organization conducts programs outside the United States, it must also abide by applicable international laws, regulations, and conventions that are legally binding on the United States.

2. A charitable organization should have a formally adopted, written code of ethics with which all of its directors or trustees, staff, and volunteers are familiar and to which they adhere.

3. A charitable organization should adopt and implement policies and procedures to ensure that all conflicts of interest, or the appearance thereof, within the organization and the board are appropriately managed through disclosure, recusal, or other means.

4. A charitable organization should establish and implement policies and procedures that enable individuals to come forward with information on illegal practices or violations or organizational policies. This "whistle-blower" policy should specify that the organization will not retaliate against, and will protect the confidentiality of, individuals who make good-faith reports.

5. A charitable organization should establish and implement policies and procedures to protect and preserve the organization's important documents and business records.

6. A charitable organization's board of directors should ensure that the organization has adequate plans to protect its assets, its property, financial and human resources, programmatic content and material, and its integrity and reputation against damage or loss. The board should review regularly the organization's needs for general liability and directors' and officers' liability insurance, as well as take other actions necessary to mitigate risks.

7. A charitable organization should make information about its operations, including its governance, finances, programs, and activities, widely available to the public. Charitable organizations also should continue making information available on the methods they use to evaluate the outcomes of their work and sharing the results of those evaluations.

### *Effective Governance*

8. A charitable organization must have a governing body that is responsible for reviewing and approving the organization's mission and strategic direction, annual budget and key financial transactions, compensation practices and policies, and fiscal and governance policies.

9. The board of a charitable organization should meet regularly enough to conduct its business and fulfill its duties.

10. The board of a charitable organization should establish its own size and structure and review these periodically. The board should have enough members to allow for full deliberation and diversity of thinking on governance and organizational matters. Except for very small organizations, this generally means that the board should have a minimum of five members.

11. The board of a charitable organization should include members with the diverse background (including, but not limited to, ethnic, racial, and gender perspectives), experience, and organizational and financial skills necessary to advance the organization's mission.

12. A substantial majority of the board of a public charity, usually meaning at least two-thirds of the members, should be independent. Independent members should not: (1) be compensated by the organization as employees or independent contractors; (2) have their compensation determined by individuals who are compensated by the organization; (3) receive, directly or indirectly, material financial benefits from the organization except as a member of the charitable class served by the

organization; or (4) be related to (as a spouse, sibling, parent, or child), or reside with any individual described above.

13. The board should hire, oversee, and annually evaluate the performance of the chief executive officer of the organization, and should conduct such an evaluation prior to any change in that officer's compensation, unless there is a multiyear contract in force or the change consists solely of routine adjustments for inflation or cost of living.

14. The board of a charitable organization that has paid staff should ensure that the positions of chief executive officer, board chair, and board treasurer are held by separate individuals. Organizations without paid staff should ensure that the positions of board chair and treasurer are held by separate individuals.

15. The board should establish an effective, systematic process for educating and communicating with board members to ensure that they are aware of their legal and ethical responsibilities, are knowledgeable about the programs and activities of the organization, and can carry out their oversight functions effectively.

16. Board members should evaluate their performance as a group and as individuals no less frequently than every three years, and should have clear procedures for removing board members who are unable to fulfill their responsibilities.

17. The board should establish clear policies and procedures addressing the length of terms and the number of consecutive terms a board member may serve.

18. The board should review organizational and governing instruments no less frequently than every five years.

19. The board should establish and review regularly the organization's mission and goals and should evaluate, no less frequently than every five years, the organization's programs, goals, and activities to be sure they advance its mission and make prudent use of its resources.

20. Board members are generally expected to serve without compensation, other than reimbursement for expenses incurred to fulfill their board duties. A charitable organization that provides compensation to its board members should use appropriate comparability data to determine the amount to be paid, document the decision, and provide full disclosure to anyone, upon request, of the amount and rationale for the compensation.

## Strong Financial Oversight

21. A charitable organization must keep complete, current, and accurate financial records. Its board should receive and review timely reports of the organization's financial activities and should have a qualified, independent financial expert audit or review these statements annually in a manner appropriate to the organization's size and scale of operations.

22. The board of a charitable organization must institute policies and procedures to ensure that the organization (and, if applicable, its subsidiaries) manages and invests its funds responsibly, in accordance with all legal requirements. The full board should review and approve the organization's annual budget and should monitor actual performance against the budget.

23. A charitable organization should not provide loans (or the equivalent, such as loan guarantees, purchasing or transferring ownership of a residence or office, or relieving a debt or lease obligation) to directors, officers, or trustees.

24. A charitable organization should spend a significant percentage of its annual budget on programs that pursue its mission. The budget should also provide sufficient resources for effective administration of the organization and, if it solicits contributions, for appropriate fundraising activities.

25. A charitable organization should establish clear, written policies for paying or reimbursing expenses incurred by anyone conducting business or traveling on behalf of the organization, including the types of expenses that can be paid for or reimbursed and the documentation required. Such policies should require that travel on behalf of the organization is to be undertaken in a cost-effective manner.

26. A charitable organization should neither pay for nor reimburse travel expenditures for spouses, dependents, or others who are accompanying someone conducting business for the organization unless they, too, are conducting such business.

## Responsible Fund-raising

27. Solicitation materials and other communications addressed to donors and the public must clearly identify the organization and be accurate and truthful.

28. Contributions must be used for purposes consistent with the donor's intent, whether as described in the relevant solicitation materials or as specified directly by the donor.

29. A charitable organization must provide donors with specific acknowledgments of charitable contributions, in accordance with IRS requirements, as well as information to facilitate the donors' compliance.

30. A charitable organization should adopt clear policies, based on its specific exempt purpose, to determine whether accepting a gift would compromise its ethics, financial circumstances, program focus, or other interests.

31. A charitable organization should provide appropriate training and supervision of the people soliciting funds on its behalf to ensure that they understand their responsibilities and applicable federal, state, and local laws and do not employ techniques that are coercive, intimidating, or intended to harass potential donors.

32. A charitable organization should not compensate internal or external fund-raisers based on a commission or a percentage of the amount raised.

33. A charitable organization should respect the privacy of individual donors and, except where disclosure is required by law, should not sell or otherwise make available the names and contact information of its donors without providing them an opportunity at least once a year to opt out of the use of their names (Panel on the Nonprofit Sector 2007, 10–48).

---

## APPENDIX 2.3A
## STRENGTHENING TRANSPARENCY, GOVERNANCE, AND ACCOUNTABILITY OF CHARITABLE ORGANIZATIONS:
### *A Final Report to Congress and the Nonprofit Sector*

*Vigorous Enforcement of Federal and State Law.* Congress should increase the amount of money that goes to the IRS and the state for oversight of tax-exempt groups.

*IRS Reporting.* IRS Forms 990, 990-EZ, and 990-PF should be improved to provide more accurate, complete, and timely information for federal and state regulators, managers of charitable organizations, and the public. Congress should impose penalties on preparers who willfully omit or misrepresent information on returns. Congress should direct the IRS to require the organization's highest-ranking officer to sign and certify the Form 990 and institute a new brief annual reporting form for organizations with less than $25,000 in annual revenues.

*Periodic Review of Tax-Exempt Status*. Instead of implementing a new periodic review system to verify that a charitable organization continues to meet the qualifications for tax exemption, the IRS should focus its resources on review and investigation of the current returns filed by charitable organizations. Boards of directors are encouraged to undertake a full review of their organization's governing documents and policies every five years.

*Financial Audits and Reviews*. Congress should require charitable organizations with at least $1 million or more in annual revenues to conduct an audit and attach audited financial statements to their Form 990 series returns and organizations with annual revenues between $250,000 and $1 million to have their financial statements reviewed by an independent public accountant.

*Disclosure of Performance Data*. Every charitable organization should, as a recommended practice, provide more detailed information about its operations, including methods it uses to evaluate the outcomes of the program, to the public through its annual report, website, and other means.

*Donor-Advised Funds*. Laws and regulations governing donor-advised funds should be strengthened to ensure that donors or related parties do not receive inappropriate benefits from these funds. Congress should amend the tax laws to define and regulate donor-advised funds. Require sponsoring charities to make minimum distributions of 5 percent of aggregate donor-advised fund assets and enforcing minimum fund activity requirements. Sponsoring charities should be prohibited from making payments to a private foundation or directly or indirectly to the fund's donors, advisers, or related parties. Tax deductions for contributions to donor-advised funds should be allowed only if the donor has a written agreement with the sponsoring charity clarifying these restrictions.

*Type III Supporting Organizations*. A Type III supporting organization should be prohibited from supporting more than five qualified entities or from supporting any organization that is controlled by the donor or a related party. It should be required to provide certain documents to, and confirm the agreement of, its supported organizations as a 501(c)(3) organization and when it files its annual Form 990 returns.

*Abusive Tax Shelters*. Congress should impose penalties on taxable participants and material advisers who fail to notify tax-exempt participants that they engaged in a "listed" and other "reportable" tax shelter.

*Non-Cash Contributions: Appreciated Property.* Congress should strengthen the rules for the appraisals that taxpayers can use to substantiate deductions claimed for property donated to charitable organizations and increase penalties for taxpayers who claim excessive deductions based on an overstated value for the donated property, as well as for appraisers who knowingly provide overstated appraisals.

*Non-Cash Contributions: Conservation and Historic Façade Easements.* Congress should increase penalties on taxpayers who claim excessive deductions for donations of conservation or historic façade easements and should permit a deduction only for an easement if it is made to a qualified charity or government entity under the terms of a written agreement that specifies the restrictions the easement imposed on future use of property. A charitable organization that accepts easement donations should be required to provide more information on its annual Form 990 about the easements it holds and to certify that it has implemented reasonable procedures for monitoring compliance with the terms of the easement agreements.

*Non-Cash Contributions: Clothing and Household Items.* Congress should not limit deductions of clothing or household items to an arbitrary ceiling. To assist taxpayers in valuation, the IRS should establish a list of the value that taxpayers can claim for specific items of clothing and household goods, based on the sale price of such items identified by major thrift store operations or other similar assessments.

*Board Compensation.* Compensation to board members of charitable organizations is discouraged. Charitable organizations that do provide compensation to board members should be required to disclose the amount and reasons for the compensation, as well as the method used to determine its reasonableness. Congress should prohibit public charities from providing loans to board members. Congress should also increase penalties on board members who receive or approve excessive compensation.

*Travel Expenses.* Charitable organizations that pay for or reimburse travel expenses of board members, officers, employees, consultants, volunteers, or others traveling to conduct business of the organization should establish and enforce policies that provide clear guidance on their travel rules, including the types of expenses that can be reimbursed and the documentation required to received reimbursement. Spouses, dependents, or others accompanying the individuals should not have their travel paid for or reimbursed by the charitable organization, unless they, too, are conducting business for the organization. Charitable organizations should be required to disclose on the Form 990 series whether they have a travel policy.

*Structure, Size, and Composition of Governing Boards.* To qualify as a 501(c)(3) tax-exempt organization, an organization should generally be required to have a minimum of three members on its governing board. To qualify as a public charity, at least one-third of the members of the governing board should be independent, meaning they have not received compensation or material benefits directly or indirectly from the organization in the previous twelve months, or whose compensation is not determined by other board or staff members, or who is not related to someone who received such compensation from the organization. Every organization should be required to disclose on its Form 990 series return which of its board members are independent. Individuals barred from service on corporate boards or convicted of crimes related to breaches of fiduciary duty should be prohibited from serving on the boards. Each charitable organization should review its board size periodically to determine the most appropriate size to ensure effective governance and to meet the organization's goals. Federal tax laws or regulations should not set a maximum number. All boards should establish strong and effective mechanisms to ensure that the board carries out its oversight functions and that board members are aware of their legal and ethical responsibilities in ensuring that the organization is governed properly.

*Audit Committee.* Governing boards should include individuals with some financial literacy. Every charitable organization that has its financial statements independently audited, whether legally required or not, should consider establishing a separate audit committee of the board. If the board does not have sufficient financial literacy and if state law permits, it may form an audit committee composed of nonstaff advisers who are not board members.

*Conflict of Interest and Misconduct.* The IRS should require every charitable organization to disclose on its Form 990 series return whether it has such a policy. Charitable organizations should also adopt policies and procedures that encourage and protect individuals who come forward with credible information on illegal practices or violations of adopted polices of the organization (Panel on the Nonprofit Sector 2005, 4–8).

## APPENDIX 2.3B
## STRENGTHENING TRANSPARENCY, GOVERNANCE, AND
## ACCOUNTABILITY OF CHARITABLE ORGANIZATIONS:
### *A Supplement to the Final Report to*
### *Congress and the Nonprofit Sector*

*International Grantmaking.* U.S.-based charitable organizations should use the Principles of International Charity to guide their work. The IRS should not institute separate or additional reporting requirements for grants to foreign grantees. No congressional action is required.

*Charitable Solicitation.* Congress should authorize funding to create a national uniform electronic filing system for charitable solicitation registration and annual reporting, but states should continue to be the primary regulators of charitable solicitation activities. The IRS should enforce the current legal prohibitions against private inurement, private benefits, and provision of excess benefits, particularly in the context of charitable solicitations. Charitable organizations should encourage the National Association of State Charity Officials (NASCO), the National Association of Attorneys General (NAAG), and the National Conference of Commissioners on Uniform State Laws (NCCUSL) to work together with the FTC, the IRS, and charitable organizations to revise and update the Model Charitable Solicitations Act to address current fund-raising vehicles and update, including the Internet. Charitable organizations should encourage state legislatures to adopt the Model Charitable Solicitations Act or other legislation designed to protect donors and punish charitable solicitation abuses.

*Compensation of Trustee of Charitable Trusts.* Congress should direct the secretary of the Treasury to: 1) amend the self-dealing regulations applicable to private foundations to clarify that when evaluating the reasonableness of a trustee's compensation, the fact that the compensation is specified in a trust instrument is not determinative of whether such compensation is excessive and 2) Amend the intermediate sanctions regulations applicable to public charities to clarify that when evaluating the reasonableness of a trustee's compensation, the fact that the compensation is specified in a trust instrument is not determinative of whether such compensation is excessive. The IRS should revise the Form 990 series returns to require that charitable organizations distinguish compensation to institutional trustees from compensation paid to individual trustees.

*Prudent Investor Standard.* Congress should direct the secretary of the Treasury to revise the Section 4944 regulations regarding jeopardizing investments, which are applicable to private foundations, to reflect the modern prudent investor standard. Congress should not enact a federal-standard care-for-investment decisions for public charities to be enforced by the IRS. Charitable organizations should work with their state legislatures to amend state laws to ensure that the modern prudent investor rule, as set forth in the Restatement of Trusts (third) and the Uniform Prudent Investor Act, is made applicable to all charitable organizations, whether formed as trusts or as corporations.

*Nonprofit Conversion Transactions.* The IRS should enforce the current legal prohibitions against private inurement, private benefits, and provision of excess benefits in the context of conversion transactions. Charitable organizations should encourage the National Association of State Charity Officials (NASCO) and the National Association of Attorneys General (NAAG) to develop guidelines regarding the appropriate role of state charity officials in nonprofit conversion transactions. States that have not done so should be encouraged to enact legislation that establishes clear notice, disclosure, and review requirements for all proposed conversions.

*Taxation on Sales of Donated Property.* Congress should amend federal tax laws to strengthen requirements for qualified appraisals used for purposes of substantiating the value of donated property as recommended by the Panel on the Nonprofit Sector in its June 2005 report.

*Consumer Credit Counseling Organization (CCO).* The IRS should continue to take action against exempt CCOs that are not operating to further a charitable or educational purpose and against organization insiders who are inappropriately using those entities for personal gain. Charitable organizations should encourage state legislatures to strengthen consumer protection statutes as needed and remove exemptions in those statutes for tax-exempt CCOs. Congress should remove current exemptions in the federal consumer protection statute for tax-exempt CCOs.

*Disclosure of Unrelated Business Activities.* The IRS should amend Form 990 to increase the information it requires about a charitable organizations unrelated business activities. Require public charities to report to the IRS any situation in which an officer, director, or trustee owns 10 percent or more of an entity in which the charity also has a 10 percent or greater ownership.

*Federal Court Equity Powers and Standing to Sue.* Congress should not expand the equity powers or jurisdiction to the Tax Court over charitable fiduciaries. Congress should not change existing law to authorize individual directors and members of the public to bring suit against charitable organizations and their directors in the Tax Court (Panel on the Nonprofit Sector 2006, 5–29).

## References

Alaimo, C.A. (2010). United Way board keeps audit confidential. *Arizona Daily Star*, April 18. http://azstarnet.com/news/local/article_1306d9dc-4651–5f3c-8fa1–22f0327d8371.html.

Allman, J.W. (2008). Costly home charge exposed. *Tampa Tribune*, November 16. www2.tbo.com/content/2008/nov/16/na-costly-home-fee-exposed/.

———. (2009). Steering allegations resurface within housing program. *Tampa Tribune*, January 20. www2.tbo.com/content/2009/jan/18/201246/na-allegations-resurface/.

BBB Wise Giving Alliance (2003). Standards for charity accountability. www.bbb.org/us/Charity-Standards/.

———. (2010). For charities and donors. www.bbb.org/us/charity.

Billitteri, T.J. (2000). Donors big and small propelled philanthropy in the 20th century. *Chronicle of Philanthropy*, January 13, 29–32.

BoardSource and Independent Sector (2006). The Sarbanes-Oxley Act and implications for nonprofit organizations. www.boardsource.org/clientfiles/sarbanes-oxley.pdf.

Carreyrou, J., and B. Martinez (2008). Grassley targets nonprofit hospitals on charity care. *Wall Street Journal*, December 18. http://online.wsj.com/article/SB122957486551517519.html.

Denhardt, K.G. (1988). *The ethics of pubic service*. New York: Greenwood Press.

Deutsch, C.H. (2005). My big fat C.E.O. paycheck. *New York Times*, April 5. www.nytimes.com/2005/04/03/business/yourmoney/03pay.html.

Ebrahim, A. (2010). The many faces of nonprofit accountability. Working Paper 10–069. Cambridge: Harvard Business School.

Eichenwald, K. (2005). Reform effort at businesses feels pressure. *New York Times*, January 14. http://query.nytimes.com/gst/fullpage.html?res=9E01E5DC1438F937A25752C0A9639C8B63.

Gibelman, M., and S. Gelman (2001). Very public scandals: Nongovernmental organizations in trouble. *Voluntas*, 12(1), 49–66.

Gibelman, M., S.R. Gelman, and D. Pollack (1997). The credibility of nonprofit boards: A view from the 1990s and beyond. *Administration in Social Work*, 21(2), 21–40.

Government Accountability Office (2007). Tax compliance. Thousands of organizations exempt from federal income tax own nearly $1 billion in payroll and other taxes. GAO Publication GAO-07–563. www.gao.gov/new.items/d07563.pdf.

Greenlee, J., M. Fischer, T. Gordon, and E. Keating (2007). An investigation of fraud in nonprofit organizations: Occurrences and deterrents. *Nonprofit and Voluntary Sector Quarterly*, 36(4), 676–694.

Grimaldi, J.V. (2007). Smithsonian documents detail chief's expenses. Invoices include work on home of Secretary Small. *Washington Post*, March 19, A01.

Grimaldi, J.V., and J. Trescott. (2007a). Former IG says Small asked her to drop audit. *Washington Post*, March 20, C01.

———. (2007b). Small's house rarely used for business. Ex-official got allowance but entertained at museums. *Washington Post*, April 19, C01.

———. (2008). Ex-director to repay Smithsonian. Report criticizes spending by Indian Museum's West. *Washington Post*, October 29, C01.

Hall, K., and E. Frazier (2008). United Way paid some salaries through in-house programs. *Charlotte Observer*, October 26. www.charlotteobserver.com/2008/10/26/279680/united-way-paid-some-salaries.html.

Harshbarger, S., and A. Crafts (2007). The whistle-blower: Policy challenges for nonprofits. *Nonprofit Quarterly*, 14(4), 36–44.

Herzlinger, R.E. (1996). Can trust in nonprofits and governments be restored? *Harvard Business Review*, March–April, 97–107.

Independent Sector and Board Source (2003, 2006). Learning from Sarbanes-Oxley: A checklist for nonprofits and foundations. www.chhsm.org/pdfs/sarbanes-oxley-checklist.pdf.

———. (2010). Code of ethics. www.independentsector.org/code_of_ethics.

Internal Revenue Service (IRS). (2009). IRS Nonprofit hospital project—final report. www.irs.gov/charities/charitable/article/0,id=203109,00.html.

Johnson, C. (2005a). Restatements up 28 percent in 2004. *Washington Post*, January 20. www.washingtonpost.com/wp-dyn/articles/A22656–2005Jan19.html.

Kinzie, S. (2010). Senators critical of salary expenses at Boys & Girls Clubs of America. *Washington Post*, March 13, A05.

National Association of Social Workers (NASW) (2008). Code of Ethics of the National Association of Social Workers. www.socialworkers.org/pubs/code/code.asp.

National Committee for Responsive Philanthropy (NCRP) (2007). David R. Jones: NCRP's board chair discusses current issues facing the sector. *NCRP Quarterly*, Spring(1), 9–12.

Olson, E. (2007a). New accusation in running of Smithsonian. *New York Times*, March 21. www.nytimes.com/2007/03/21/us/21museum.html.

———. (2007b). Embattled Smithsonian official resigns. *New York Times*, March 27. www.nytimes.com/2007/03/27/arts/27museum.html.

Ottaway, D. B., and J. Stephens (2003). Nonprofit land bank amasses billions. Charity builds assets on corporate partnerships. *Washington Post*, May 4, A01.

Panel on the Nonprofit Sector (2005). Strengthening the transparency, governance, and accountability of charitable organizations: A final report to Congress and the nonprofit sector. www.nonprofitpanel.org/report/final/.

———. (2006). Strengthening the transparency, governance, and accountability of charitable organizations: A supplement to the final report to Congress and the nonprofit sector. April. www.nonprofitpanel.org/Report/supplement/Panel_Supplement_Final.pdf.

———. (2007). Principles for good governance and ethical practice: A guide for charities and foundations. October. www.nonprofitpanel.org/report/principles/Principles_Guide.pdf.

Perry, S. (2008). Public confidence in nonprofit groups slide back, new survey finds. *Chronicle of Philanthropy*, 20(12) (April 8), 12.

Salmon, J.L. (2006). United Way official resigns, alleges inflated numbers. *Washington Post*, May 22, B01.

Shrives, L. (2010). Are nonprofit hospitals truly not for profit? *Orlando Sentinel*, July 31. http://articles.orlandosentinel.com/2010–07–31/news/os-nonprofit-hospitals-20100731_1_charity-care-nonprofit-hospitals-community-benefit-programs.

Stamler, B. (2004). After a spate of scandals, a debate on new rules. *New York Times*, November 25, F25.

Stephens, J., and D.B. Ottaway (2003a). Nonprofit sells scenic acreage to allies at a loss: Buyers gain tax breaks with few curbs on and use. *Washington Post*, May 6, A01.

———. (2003b). Nature Conservancy suspends land sales. *Washington Post*, May 13. A03.

———. (2003c). 12 home loans at Conservancy. Nonprofit says all but 2 have been repaid; 5 came interest-free. *Washington Post*, June 13. A08.

———. (2005). Senators question Conservancy's practices. *Washington Post*, June 8. A03.

Strom, S. (2002a). Senator questions finances of United Way. *New York Times*, August 22. www.nytimes.com/2002/08/22/us/senator-questions-finances-of-united-way.html.

———. (2002b). Questions arise on accounting at United Way. *New York Times*, November 19. www.nytimes.com/2002/11/19/business/questions-arise-on-accounting-at-united-way.html.

———. (2009). IRS study tried to assess if hospitals earn tax breaks. *New York Times*, February 13. A17.

Subcommittee Chairman's Report to Subcommittee No. 1, Select Committee on Small Business 1962–1972. See "Tax-Exempt Foundations and Charitable Trusts: Their Impact on the Economy," *Subcommittee Chairman's Report to Subcommittee No. 1, Select Committee on Small Business*, House of Representatives. The items included are dated December 31, 1962, October 16, 1963, March 20, 1964, December 21, 1966, April 28, 1967, March 26, 1968, June 30, 1969, and August 1972.

Trescott, J. (2008). Smithsonian strategies suggested. GAO calls for method of measuring reforms after 2007 spending scandals. *Washington Post*, May 16, C04.

U.S. Senate Committee on Finance 1965. Treasury Department Report on Private Foundations. 89th Congress 1st session.

Veiga, J.F. (2004). Bringing ethics into the mainstream: An introduction to the special topic. *Academy of Management Executive*, 18(2), 37–38.

Whitaker, G.P., F.S. Bluestein, A.R. Brown-Graham, L. Altman-Sauer, and M. Henderson (2003). Accountability in local government-nonprofit relationships. *IQ Report*, 35 (5). Washington, DC: ICMA.

Zongker, B. (2007). Smithsonian chief resigns amid criticism. *Washington Post*, March 26. www.washingtonpost.com/wp-dyn/content/article/2007/03/26/AR2007032600665.html.

———. (2008). Smithsonian to make large cuts to executives' pay. *USA Today*, August 29. www.usatoday.com/news/nation/2008–08–29–3348426537_x.htm.

# ─── 3 ───

# Nonprofit Governance

Nonprofit organizations are governed by a board of directors. It is the responsibility of the directors to make sure that the *public purpose* of the nonprofit organization is executed. The board of directors or board of trustees of a nonprofit organization makes policy and provides oversight. The duties and authority of nonprofit governing boards are regulated by the organization's bylaws. Unlike for-profit boards of directors whose priorities are profits and returns to stockholders, nonprofit board members are obligated to act in a way that reflects the values and mission of the nonprofit and represents the public interest (Hodgkin 1993; Jeavons 1992; Young 2002).

Accountability for any nonprofit ultimately rests with its board. Although the board may delegate management authority to a paid staff person, typically the executive director, the board of directors can never be relieved of its legal and fiduciary responsibilities. A fiduciary is a person or institution given the power to act on the administration, investment, and distribution of property that belongs to someone else. Board members are stewards of the public interest and have a burden of responsibility to use and preserve the organization's assets for advancing its public mission. The most critical work of any governing board is to create and re-create the reason for the organization's existence and the production of worthwhile results (Carver 1990). Unfortunately, the governing boards of many nonprofits have fallen short in executing their oversight responsibilities. Consider the following examples:

**1. Smithsonian's National Museum of the American Indian:**
W. Richard West Jr., who retired as director in 2007 from the Smithsonian's National Museum of the American Indian (NMAI), was investigated for extravagant expenditures. Sixty percent of his travel lacked documentation, and there was no oversight of the receipts to see if the travel expenses were justified. More than $250,000 in institution funds was spent over the previous four years on premium transportation and plush lodgings in hotels around the world (Grimaldi and Trescott 2008a, 2008b).

**2. Oral Roberts University:** Richard Roberts, the son of founder Oral Roberts, was forced to resign as the president of Oral Roberts University after it became public that he used university money for shopping sprees, home improvements, and a stable of horses for his daughters at a time when the university was more than $50 million in debt. In November 2008, the university laid off 100 employees after it agreed to a nearly $450,000 separation with its former president (Blumenthal 2007; Kovach 2007; Associated Press 2008a, 2008b).

**3. The Nature Conservancy:** The Nature Conservancy came under scrutiny after investing in a number of for-profit businesses, leaving the organization with a $24 million debt. It also entered into financial transactions and bought land and services from companies run by its board members and state and regional trustees. The Nature Conservancy extended housing loans to executives at interest rates ranging from zero to 6.02 percent (Stephens and Ottaway 2003a, 2003b, 2003c, 2003d, 2005).

These examples demonstrate some of the conflicts of interest that can arise between the actions of a board of directors and what is in the best interests of a nonprofit organization. This chapter discusses the oversight roles and responsibilities of boards of directors and the context in which they operate. As you read this chapter, reflect on the following questions and why understanding them can result in improved agency effectiveness.

- How can the board of directors assist the nonprofit agency in meeting its current challenges?
- What style of board involvement is appropriate for your nonprofit agency?
- How can the strategies and procedures for nominating and selecting board members be updated to address the current needs of your nonprofit agency?
- Should the management competencies of the executive director influence the types of individuals and their skills to be selected as board members? Should this determine the governance style of the board of directors?
- How can board practices lead to effective and professional organizational performance?

## Board Roles and Responsibilities

It is the board of directors' responsibility to determine the organization's mission and see that the organization fulfills its obligation. The board is responsible for ensuring that the organization is well run. The board determines which programs are the most consistent with the organization's mission and monitors their effectiveness.

The board selects the executive, supports the executive, and reviews the executive's performance. Prior to selecting the executive, it is the board's responsibility to develop the chief executive's job description, develop the selection criteria to be utilized, determine the appropriate compensation, and develop a recruitment plan to find the most qualified individual. The board should ensure that the chief executive has the professional staff support needed to further the goals of the organization. In partnership with the executive, the board should agree upon the evaluation criteria and the review period.

As stewards of the organization, boards must actively participate with the staff in the planning process and assist in implementing the plan's goals by ensuring that the organization has adequate resources. This can be accomplished by fund-raising activities, such as serving as an advocate with funding sources (foundation, corporation, government entity, federated fund-raising organizations such as the United Way), making personal contributions, organizing a fund-raising event, hosting a benefit, or through the face-to-face solicitation of other individuals.

The board provides oversight and sees that the organization's resources are managed effectively. To remain accountable to its donors, funders, and the public, and to safeguard its tax-exempt status, the board must assist in developing the annual budget and ensure that proper financial controls are in place. The board must also see that human resources and infrastructure resources are managed effectively.

The board is a link to the community. Directors should articulate the organization's mission, accomplishments, and goals to the public. Often, directors are chosen to bring the experience or perspective of a particular group or segment of the organization's constituency to the board.

The board is responsible for ensuring that the organization meets legal requirements and that it is operating in accordance with its mission for the purpose for which it was granted tax-exemption.

By evaluating its performance in fulfilling its responsibilities, the board can recognize its achievements and reach consensus on which areas need to be improved.

## Standards of Conduct

There are recognized standards of conduct for board members. *Duty of Care* imposes an obligation that board members discharge their duties with the care that an ordinary prudent person would exercise under similar circumstances. This includes attending meetings, becoming acquainted with issues before reaching a decision, reading financial statements, asking questions, keeping the organization current in regard to legal obligations. It refers to the responsibility to pay attention to what is going on and make decisions based on good information. Directors are liable for making sure that the nonprofit is carrying out its mission as articulated to both the state and federal governments. Donors, in particular, should be able to expect that their funds are used for the purposes for which the organization is established.

*Duty of Loyalty* requires that each board member act primarily in the best interest of the organization. The interest of the organization comes before the interests of the directors when making decisions. A violation of this standard occurs when a director's personal financial interest is put ahead of the nonprofit's, using corporate property for personal purposes, taking advantage of a financial opportunity at the expense of the nonprofit, or any kind of self-dealing without proper disclosure is generally not permitted by law.

*Duty of Obedience* imposes an obligation that directors will act in conformiy with all laws, in addition to acting in accordance with the organization's mission.

## Board Liability

The subject of board liability involves state laws, which vary from state to state. However, some generalizations can be made. Directors are liable only for gross negligence and, according to the language of many statutes, need only exhibit "such care as an ordinary *prudent* person in a like position would use under similar circumstances." Directors are not typically liable for business judgments or financial decisions if they show no conflict of interest and do not appear irrational. A financial decision that has an undesirable outcome or one that involves a high degree of risk is not sufficient grounds to hold directors liable. However, if directors do not attend meetings, if they approve major decisions involving the nonprofit's financial resources without conducting research on any background financial information, or if they engage in any illegal financial activity, they can be held liable.

Directors are expected to make sure that their organizations comply with the rules and regulations set by federal, state, and local governments. Nonprofits must file financial reports with the IRS and with the state office handling nonprofits as well as deduct taxes from paychecks, and deposit these funds. Directors can be held personally and financially liable for noncompliance with tax requirements. In some cases, directors can be held responsible for the organization's compliance with laws limiting lobbying activities. Where a building is involved, they can be held responsible for making sure the organization is complying with building codes. It is essential to remember that as stewards of the public trust, the directors are responsible for overseeing compliance with legal requirements.

### Minimizing Risk

Nonprofit organizations can attempt to minimize the personal risk of directors by indemnifying their directors. Indemnification ensures that the nonprofit will pay the reasonable costs associated with liability suits such as judgments and settlements against board members. This *does not protect the directors from legal action.* But it does mean that the organization will pay for all costs associated with such actions against the directors, including the cost of settlement. The problem with indemnification is that it transfers risk from the directors to the organization and puts the organization's assets at risk. Another problem is that in certain cases, the organization may sue one of its directors and, if successful, would not be responsible for paying the costs associated with indemnification.

Directors and officers (D&O) insurance protects both against indemnification costs and any other costs incurred by directors that would not be covered by the nonprofit. This type of insurance contract agrees to pay, on behalf of the directors and officers of the organization, financial losses that arise from claims or lawsuits brought against them for committing some wrongful act. A wrongful act is generally defined as an actual or alleged error, omission, wrong or misleading statement, or neglect or breach of duty in the governance or management of the organization.

The Volunteer Protection Act of 1997 indicates that no person serving without compensation as director, officer, or trustee of a 501(c)(3) nonprofit organization shall be liable to any other person based solely on his or her conduct in the execution of such office unless the conduct constitutes gross negligence, was intentionally harmful, or was not within the scope of the volunteer activity, or if the volunteer was not properly licensed. This limited immunity does not preclude the need for D&O insurance. These amendments to the non-for-profit corporation laws contain a number of exceptions. If a lawsuit is brought, legal expenses will be incurred to present motions to the courts to dismiss the actions; a complaint based on gross negligence or intentional infliction of harm will likely not be dismissed; the organization itself and any staff named in the complaint will not be protected by this immunity. Without insurance, an organization and its directors and officers can spend many years and many thousands of dollars in disposing of such claims and lawsuits, even if they eventually win. Often the organization's bylaws will have a provision to indemnify and defend its directors and officers from such claims and lawsuits. While this is advisable, it does not preclude the need for D&O insurance to reimburse and/or protect the organization from financial costs associated with such claims.

Because all of these measures protect only the directors themselves, the nonprofit should carry sufficient liability insurance to protect itself in the case of a lawsuit.

### Responsibilities of Individual Board Members

The responsibilities of individual directors include attending all board of directors meetings and assigned committee meetings and functions, as well as attending special events.

Directors need to be informed and stay abreast of the nonprofit's mission, services, policies, and programs. Meeting agendas and supporting materials should be reviewed prior to board and committee meetings. When asked, directors should be willing to serve on committees and offer to take on special assignments.

Directors should be expected to make a personal financial contribution to the organization. Some nonprofits have a minimum dollar amount that must be donated, others allow their directors to contribute what they can afford, still others will accept in-kind donations in lieu of a direct financial donation. Many funders, whether foundations, public agencies, or federated fund-raising organizations like United Way of America affiliates, want to see 100 percent of board directors contributing to the nonprofit. If the directors are not committed to the agency and support its mission, then why should funders?

Directors should keep up-to-date on developments in the nonprofit's field and inform others about the organization. Directors should be on the lookout for potential directors who can make significant contributions to the work of the board and the organization. Each director should follow conflict of interest and confidentiality policies and assist the board in carrying out its fiduciary and legal responsibilities.

*How do you stay out of trouble?* Become an active board member, attend all meetings, insist on having sound financial management tools and control systems in place, speak up—ask questions, don't remain silent, and identify any conflicts of interest.

Directors, like other volunteers, should be evaluated on their performance and the contributions they make to the nonprofit. Directors who miss meetings or are unprepared when they do attend should be held accountable. The fiduciary and oversight responsibilities of governing boards necessitate having individuals who are committed to the agency for the length of their board terms of office. Organizations cannot afford to retain board members who ignore their responsibilities. The board as a whole should also assess how it is carrying out its duties.

### Size and Composition of the Board

The nonprofit's charter and bylaws state the number of directors required. State laws usually set a minimum. Florida State law requires that a nonprofit corporation's board of directors include at least three officers: a president (or chairperson), a treasurer, and a clerk (or secretary). Some organizations include additional officers, such as a vice president or an assistant treasurer. The organization's bylaws will specify how many officers there must be, their titles, powers, and duties. The bylaws will also state the process by which they are elected and the frequency of the elections.

The *president* presides at board meetings, appoints committee chairpersons, works closely with the executive director to guide the organization, and often acts as its public spokesman. The *treasurer* oversees the organization's financial standing, makes regular financial reports to the board, and serves as chairperson of the board's finance committee. The *secretary/clerk* oversees the nonprofit's documentation, records board meeting minutes, and distributes minutes and announcements of upcoming meetings to directors. The minutes constitute the official and binding record of board decisions. Some nonprofit bylaws specify additional officer positions. A *vice president* may preside at board meetings in the president's absence and serves as a committee chairperson as appointed by the president.

## Skills and Areas of Knowledge

A board must collectively possess skills and knowledge that relate to its responsibilities identified earlier: planning, finance and accounting, fund-raising (including business/corporate, individual, public agency, and foundation), human resources management, marketing and public relations, and legal expertise, especially relating to nonprofit corporations. Some directors should also be familiar with the programs and activities that the organization sponsors, and all directors should support the organization's mission. Directors should represent a variety of backgrounds as well as various segments of the community, including different minority and ethnic groups that will give the board a broad vision and understanding of the true meaning of community and public service. In addition, specific nonprofits may require directors with other types of expertise and representation. For example, if a nonprofit corporation owns a facility, operates a building, or maintains extensive grounds, it may be desirable to have an architect or a contractor on the board. Much of the work of the board of directors is done through committees.

## Types of Board Committees

The *Executive Committee* is generally empowered to act for the full board in matters that require immediate action or do not involve major questions of policy or funding. Often, the members of the executive committee are the officers of the board. Sometimes an organization's bylaws empower the executive committee to make decisions on behalf of the full board in an emergency or in other special circumstances when the full board cannot be convened.

The *Finance Committee* assists the treasurer in overseeing financial activities and making budgets. This committee is usually headed by the treasurer. It hires the auditing firm and reviews the audit results. Typically, an accountant is recruited for this committee.

The *Development Committee* sets fund-raising goals and plans for fund-raising activities for the organization. Sometimes referred to as the Fund-Raising Committee, it oversees the planning and coordination of fund-raising efforts.

The *Nomination Committee* recruits new board members and nominates board officers for election to their positions. Typical responsibilities include identifying, vetting, and recommending prospective directors.

The *Program Committee* reviews the nonprofit's programs and plans ahead. This committee works closely with staff, and its members typically have some expertise in the area.

The *Planning Committee* coordinates long-range planning for the nonprofit.

The *Human Resources Management (HRM) Committee* develops HRM policies, and handle grievances when board involvement is necessary. In some nonprofits, the HRM committee develops or recommends the performance evaluation instrument to use when evaluating the chief executive to the board. The HRM committee may also be responsible for determining other HRM studies or needs.

The *Marketing* or *Public Relations Committee* develops marketing and/or public relations plans for the nonprofit.

Some nonprofits have an *Advisory Council* of individuals who have special skills or talents but may not be able to make the commitment that a director position requires. As an advisory council member, individuals are asked to contribute their knowledge and skills on an ad-hoc basis. Their expertise, skill, experience, capital, and celebrity are typically assembled to supplement the governance activities carried out by governing boards or the management tasks carried out by staff members. They might provide a specialized expertise that is missing from your board or staff. The members may not have time to be board members nor want the fiduciary responsibilities but are willing to assist in specific projects. They have been used to survey the need for new programs, review applications for funding, make resource allocation recommendations, raise funds, and conduct evaluation and oversight activities. At times they might help organizations maintain accountability or meet the demands of an external constituency. Members of advisory councils can be ambassadors to the community and connect nonprofits with a greater variety of constituents. They can also assist in fund-raising and program management (Axelrod 2004, 2–3).

The size and type of the nonprofit will determine the extent of board committees. Committees should exist when there is a need for them. A larger board typically allows for greater representation and a larger base of donors and fund-raisers; however, a larger number of directors often allows directors to assume less responsibility and be less engaged in oversight functions.

## Recruiting Directors

What should an organization look for in its directors? Some organizational theories have been used to explain different models for selecting board members.

### *Resource Dependency Theory*

Resource dependency theory suggests that an organization's behavior is dependent upon its ability to garner the resources it needs to function and survive. In seeking resources, organizations will respond to and become reliant on those entities that control resources. Their success will depend on their abilities to manage the dependency and negotiate external demands. The ability to acquire and maintain needed resources is essential to the agency's survival. Because no organization controls all of the resources it needs to survive, the board plays a crucial role in facilitating an exchange that reduces interdependences of the organization's operating environment. Board members, through their personal or professional associations, provide benefits to the organization because they can access relevant information and thereby reduce uncertainty. In the context of nonprofit organizations, resource dependency theory suggests that the board is likely to recruit members who can facilitate access to critical criteria used to evaluate the organization. The board links the organization with its environment so that influential others deem the organization effective and continue to provide the resources necessary for survival. Hodge and Piccolo (2005) found a relationship between funding source, board involvement, and financial vulnerability. Consistent with resource dependency theory, the funding sources of nonprofits have an influence on strategy implementation and on performance when measured by financial vulnerability in the face of economic uncertainty.

Board members of nonprofits that rely more on private funding tend to be more involved than the board members of nonprofits who are more reliant on government funds.

## Agency Theory

Agency theory stresses the importance of separating ownership from control. Board members have the responsibility to select and evaluate chief executives and monitor their actions to ensure that the best interests of management are aligned to not conflict with the interests of the organization or society. Agency theory predicts that nonprofit boards select members capable of providing organizational oversight. New members monitor administrative actions to ensure that the interests of management are properly aligned with constituent expectations (Miller-Millesen 2003).

## Institutional Theory

Institutional theory focuses attention on the ways in which organizational structure and processes reflect institutional pressures, rules, norms, and sanctions because these activities and courses of action have become the accepted way of doing things (DiMaggio and Powell 1983; Meyer and Rowan 1977). This theory is useful in understanding why many nonprofit boards engage in similar activities, codify like practices, and develop related structures. According to institutional theory, new board members are people who can legitimize the organization. Board composition reflects institutional pressures to conform to community expectations.

Institutional isomorphism suggests that organizational changes result from processes that make organizations within a highly structured organizational field more homogenous, but not necessarily more efficient. An organizational field becomes "institutionally defined: through the increased interaction among organizations in the field, the emergence of formal participants in the organizational field that they belong to is a common enterprise (DiMaggio and Powell 1983, 148). Once an organizational field has been defined, organizations within this field will frame changes in accordance with the established norms of the field; thus, organizations may try to change constantly but are constrained from doing so and are influenced to adopt institutionalized practices. In adopting these institutionalized practices, they tend to become isomorphic with their environments (Meyer and Rowan 1977). Institutional isomorphism provides organizations with legitimacy and promotes survival, since organizational elements of formal structure have been legitimated externally, meaning that organizations do not need to provide evidence of efficiency or use internal assessment to define the value of these elements (ibid.).

Abzug and Galaskiewicz (2001) note that the boards of nonprofits provide important governance and legitimacy functions. Stakeholders cannot know if nonprofits are faithful to their mission or use funds wisely, so they judge the organization by seeing who is on its board. Boards come to represent the organization and become a basis for its legitimacy claims. The board composition is important. Neo-institutional theory organizations restructure themselves and adopt certain practices to conform to dominant ideologies, beliefs, fads, norms, and regulations. This ensures their legitimacy. Applied to a nonprofit board, the credentials and expertise of trustees are one way to communicate the organization's allegiance to efficiency norms and business models. The political sociology, social movement literature talks about organizational legitimacy in terms of constituent support. An organization is legitimate if it represents the interests or identities of different constituents in the community. Rather than deriving their legitimacy from the state—the professional and institutional gatekeepers—the organization gains legitimacy from the community.

## Nonprofits Are Different

Training and orientation are important for all board members regardless of their professional expertise and experience. William Novelli, the former CEO of AARP, notes that many business executives do not understand the context of the nonprofit environment. "Nonprofit goals are more complex and more intangible. It may be hard to compete in the filed of consumer packaged goods or electronics or high finance, but it is harder to achieve goals in the nonprofit world, because these goals tend to be behavioral. If you set out to do something about breast cancer in this country, or about social security solvency, it's a hell of a lot harder to pull that off. And it's also harder to measure" (cited in Silverman and Taliento 2006, 37).

Drawing on previous research on board members' motivation to serve, Inglis and Cleave (2006) developed a scale to assess board members' motivations. They identified six components: enhancing self-worth, learning through community, helping the community, developing individual relationships, unique contributions to the board, and self-healing. *Enhancing self-worth* reflects attitudes and behaviors that benefit the individuals serving as board members; *learning through community* benefits the individual's growth through learning new skills, learning about the community, developing strengths, and making contacts; *helping the community* reflect motivations to make a difference; *developing individual relationships* reflects the importance of social relationships with fellow board members; *unique contributions to the board* addresses what individuals perceive to be the skills or knowledge they bring to the board; and *self-healing* considers why individuals might be interested in volunteering as a way to deal positively with deeply felt needs.

## Risk Management

Risk management is the means by which an organization can identify, assess, and control risks that may be present within its board, staffing, organizational structure, operations, and relations with the community. In a nonprofit context, the organization identifies potential risk in its operations by examining the quality of internal controls, safety, and actions of its staff and volunteers on the job. Critical components of a risk management strategy include the following:

- *Risk Assessment.* The step that determines what risks are present in the nonprofit and their potential severity
- *Risk Management Strategy Implementation.* The risks identified in the assessment stage are addressed through one or more of the following risk treatments:
- *Avoidance.* This means discontinuing the activity or practice.
- *Retention.* When a program, service, or activity cannot be eliminated, the nonprofit either establishes a restricted fund that would be used to address losses from the risk, or it significantly raises the deductible on an insurance policy that addresses the risk.
- *Modification.* This method addresses how the features of a risk can be changed to reduce its potential for frequency or severity.

- *Transfer.* The most common way to transfer the financial aspects of the risk is to purchase insurance or to hire another organization to provide a high-risk service.

- *Monitoring for Results.* The nonprofit needs to evaluate whether or not the chosen strategy is effective.

The types of risks that directors and nonprofits must anticipate may possibly include:

- *Property:* tangible property, intangible property, financial impact of cost to replace, loss of income.
- *Income:* decreases in revenues, increases in expenses, property losses, people losses, reputation losses.
- *Liability:* performance of contractual promises; personal safety of staff, clients, customers, and volunteers; protection of property; security of reputation; and risks that may be related to vulnerable populations such as the elderly, disabled, and children (Jackson 2006).

Directors are responsible for verifying that the nonprofit has undertaken a risk management assessment and has developed strategies to deal with possible risks.

There are many excellent resources for information on a board of directors (see references at the end of the chapter), but what tends to be lacking is information on how boards should govern and how effective boards are.

**Really, Are Boards Effective?**

The Urban Institute's Center on Nonprofits and Philanthropy surveyed 5,100 nonprofit organizations of various sizes, types, and locations (Ostrower 2007). The study had three major purposes: investigate the relationship between the public policy environment and nonprofits, given the Sarbanes-Oxley Act's requirement that for-profit corporate boards strengthen their governance and deter fraud; identify factors associated with promoting or impeding boards' performance of basic stewardship responsibilities related to oversight, and supporting the organization and its mission; and draw greater attention to board composition and recruitment processes. Ostrower (2007, 12) found that the greater scrutiny of for-profit boards prompted nonprofits to revisit and reassess policies for greater oversight. The survey asked how active boards are in the duties typically ascribed to them, such as fund-raising, financial oversight, evaluating the chief executive, planning for the future, setting organizational policy, monitoring programs and policies, community relations, educating the public about the organization and its mission, monitoring the board's own performance, and acting as a sounding board for management. Fifty-two percent said they were active in setting organizational policy and financial oversight.

Among nonprofits with a paid professional chief executive, 54 percent of the respondents said their boards were very engaged in evaluating the chief executive; 29 percent of the respondents said their board was very active in fund-raising; 32 percent said their board was very active in monitoring the organization's programs and services; 17 percent noted that their board was very active in monitoring the board's own performance; 44 percent said the board was active in planning for the future; 27 percent noted that the board was very active in community relations; and 23 percent noted that their board was very active in educating the public about the organization and its mission.

In regard to board composition, the results indicated on average 86 percent of board members are white non-Hispanic; 7 percent are African American or black; 3.5 percent are Hispanic/Latino; and the balance reflects other ethnic groups. Board practices and policies that are positively associated with having minority-group members on boards include diversified funding sources, percentage of women on the board, board size, a national geographic scope, and the importance of racial and ethnic diversity as a board recruitment criterion.

In regard to gender, 94 percent of the nonprofit boards responding to the survey include women, and they are almost balanced with respect to gender. On average, boards are composed of 46 percent women. The percentage of women is inversely related to organizational size: 50 percent among nonprofits with expenses under $100,000 but dropping to a low of 29 percent among the largest nonprofits with over $40 million in expenses. Factors positively associated with the percentage of women on boards include the percentage of clientele served by the nonprofit that are female, funding sources, percent of funding from government and foundations, term limits, a local or regional geographical focus, placing importance on willingness to give time, knowledge of the organization's mission area, racial and ethnic diversity as a recruitment criteria, and organizational age.

The percentage of nonprofit directors that serve on corporate boards ranged from 31 percent among the smallest nonprofits to 8 percent among the larger ones. Most board members were employed. Of those employed, on average more than 55 percent worked for a business, another 18 percent were self-employed, 12 percent worked for another nonprofit, 11 percent worked for government, and 3 percent worked for the nonprofit itself.

Forty-one percent of the respondents noted that the ages of their board ranged between 50 and 65; 37 percent of nonprofit boards had directors between 36 and 50. On average only 16 percent of board members are older than 65, and 7 percent are under 36. Most of the respondents recognized the need to recruit younger board members.

The study found that oversight and accountability dominated board agendas and that the boards needed to give greater attention to performance. A substantial percentage of boards were not actively engaged in various basic governance activities. The research also found a level of insularity among nonprofit boards not consistent with their mandate to serve the public interest. Most boards had high levels of racial and ethnic homogeneity. The research also suggests that the failure to engage in community relations may contribute to boards' seeming lack of awareness of potential public reaction to some of the controversial practices and decisions that have been widely publicized in various scandals.

## Select Earlier Research on Governing Boards

Previous research on nonprofit boards found that various stakeholders such as chief executives, funders, and trustees perceived board effectiveness to be the most important determinant of perceived organizational effectiveness (Herman and Renz 2000).

### Policy as Governance

John Carver believes that boards should govern proactively through statements of values rather than being reactive or by making event-specific decisions. Leadership should be exerted through policies the board develops. Policy leadership should clarify, inspire, and set a tone of discourse. The board should espouse values about *ends*, what results, benefits, or changes are worth what costs; what staff practices would be considered unacceptable; *board–staff linkages*, how power is passed and accountability evaluated; and *board process*, how the board will govern and on whose behalf. The role of the board is to examine the policy implications of any initiatives it is asked to approve and to rise above the technical complexity by being a guardian of values (1990, 29–35).

### Competencies Are Important

Richard P. Chait (2003) notes that there is a line between management and governance. The board supports the executive and sets performance expectations, however, the executive is responsible for the day-to-day activities. Board meetings should be structured to direct the board's attention to matters of policy and strategy. For a board to be effective, it needs to develop competencies in these areas:

- *Contexual:* The board understands and takes into account the culture, norms, and values of the organization it governs.
- *Educational:* The board takes the necessary steps to ensure that members are well informed about the organization, the profession, and the board's own roles, responsibilities, and performance.
- *Interpersonal:* The board nurtures the development of its members as a group, attends to the board's collective welfare, and fosters a sense of cohesiveness.
- *Analytical:* The board recognizes complexities and subtleties in the issues and facts and draws on multiple perspectives to dissect complex problems and synthesize appropriate responses.
- *Political:* The board accepts as one of its primary responsibilities the need to develop and maintain healthy relationships among all key constituencies.
- *Strategic:* The board envisions and shapes institutional direction and helps to ensure a strategic approach to the organization's future.

### Governance as Leadership

In the book titled *Governance as Leadership: Reframing the Work of Nonprofit Boards,* Chait et al. (2005) identify three modes of governance that compose governance as leadership.

*Type I* is the fiduciary mode, where boards are concerned primarily with the stewardship of tangible assets. Boards review audits, investments, compensation, facilities, fund-raising, and executive performance and enactment of policies and practices that discourage waste, prevent abuse, or promote efficiency. Type I boards provide more of an oversight role. The authors believe that this style of governance describes only the bureaucratic dimensions of organizations and does not explain how modern nonprofits actually operate. They claim "too much governing and too little leadership" (p. 35).

*Type II* boards are more strategic. Type II boards create a strategic partnership with management. They ask questions and come up with ideas, focusing on the big picture. Type II boards rely more on subcommittees and task forces that convene when needed and disband when appropriate (p. 73). Together, the board and management identify strategic priorities and drivers from multiple sources. Flexibility is an important component, and the board structure mirrors organizational strategic priorities.

*Type III* boards provide generative thinking, a sense of what knowledge, information, and data mean. It is the process of framing problems. "Generative thinking is where goal-setting and direction-setting originate" (p. 89). Generative thinking has been referred to by other scholars as adaptive leadership, reflective practice, sense-making, and emergent strategy. Directors and the executive collaborate to initiate and oversee generative work such as questioning assumptions, probing feasibility, and identifying obstacles and opportunities.

According to this theory, when trustees work well in all three of these modes, the board achieves governance as leadership (pp. 6–7). Type I and II are the most dominant modes of nonprofit governance, and Type III is the least practiced.

## Conclusion

Designing effective governance structures and processes has been an issue for a long time and continues to garner a lot of attention. Reviews of the literature outline the complexities and difficulties surrounding internal governance structures and practices. Likewise, many of the authors and scholars noted above identified the need for governing boards to change how they understand and implement their responsibilities. As the external environment of nonprofits is becoming more complex, directors are struggling with the engagement and accountability demanded. Care must be taken to balance the legitimate and sometimes conflicting interests of differing constituencies. Decision-making should be inclusive and deliberative in its approach (Hodgkin 1993).

Nonprofits designated as public charities exist primarily to serve the public at large rather than members of the organizations. The rationale for permitting donors to enjoy the benefits of tax deductibility is that these organizations are thought to serve broad public purposes that transcend the personal interests of their members and benefactors. Boards of directors are responsible for developing policies and providing the necessary oversight and guidance to facilitate ethical and professional management of nonprofits.

---

### Case 3.1. Did a Montana Museum Board Breach Its Duty?

The Montana Supreme Court dismissed the board of the Charles M. Bair Family Museum in Martinsdale, Montana, saying it breached its fiduciary duties by closing the museum in 2002.

The museum was financed by a trust created by Alberta M. Bair. The trust stated it "was her cherished aim and foremost desire" to establish a museum in the Bair family house. She directed the board to spend whatever was necessary from the trust's principal and interest to maintain the museum and to buy property if needed. She also gave the board the option of closing the museum after five years. The board members said that attendance had declined, the house was ill-suited to be a museum, and it lacked adequate security and protection against fire as the collection increased in value. From 2002 to 2005, the value of just the art collection increased by 40 percent. Some of the most valuable pieces were moved to other institutions at the board's discretion, reducing the attraction, and the court did not order their return.

The court ruled that the board had not spent enough money to give it a good start. The museum was home to an eclectic collection of fine European antiques, valuable artworks, and priceless Indian artifacts. It ordered U.S. Bank, the trustee, to create a new board. "As a result of the board's failure to spend 'whatever principal and income of the Charles M. Bair Family Trust that is necessary to improve and maintain the museum,' the museum never received a fair opportunity to succeed; the museum was destined for failure rather than success," the court wrote in its opinion, quoting the trust documents. "The board's ensuing breaches emanated from this initial failure."

The case had been watched by the nonprofit world and state regulators of charities. The regulators are often responsible for interpreting and defending donors' intentions long after their deaths and in the face of strong opposition from powerful boards. Thirteen states filed amicus briefs in support of the Montana attorney general.

*Source:* Strom and Robbins 2008.

---

### Case 3.2. When Is Nonprofit Executive Pay Too High?

The Montgomery County Council has withheld $55,000 in county funding for Food & Friends, a Washington, D.C., nonprofit that delivers meals to people living with HIV/AIDS and cancer, because its executive director made $357,447 in salary and benefits in 2007. According to IRS records, Food & Friends' budget was more than $9.7 million in 2007.

As a result, 8,000 specialized meals and nutrition counseling will not be funded by the Montgomery County government. The president of the board of directors said the agency hired a "nationally recognized independent consultant" to come up with the executive director's salary and that the salary was frozen this year because of the poor economy. County council staff noted that the county received applications for grants from about 150 organizations, about two-thirds of which did not have any staff members who made more than $100,000.

*Source:* Suderman 2009.

---

### References

Abzug, R., and J. Galaskiewicz (2001). Nonprofit boards: Crucibles of expertise or symbols of local identities? *Nonprofit and Voluntary Sector Quarterly*, 30(1), 51–73.

Associated Press (2008a). Oklahoma: Oral Roberts settlement. October 24.

———. (2008b). Oral Roberts to lay off 100 employees. November 18.

Axelrod, N.R. (2004). *Advisory councils*. Rev. ed. Washington, DC: BoardSource.

Baker, J.R. (1994). Government in the twilight zone: Motivations of volunteers to small city boards and commissions. *State and Local Government Review*, 26, 119–128.

Blumenthal, R. (2007). President of Oral Roberts to take leave of absence. *New York Times*, October 18. www.nytimes.com/2007/10/18/us/18oral.html.

Carver, J. (1990). *Boards that make a difference*. San Francisco: Jossey-Bass.

Chait, R.P. (2003). *How to help your board govern more and manage less*. Rev. ed. Washington, DC: BoardSource.

Chait, R.P., W.P. Ryan, and B.E. Taylor (2005). *Governance as leadership: Reframing the work of nonprofit boards*. Hoboken, NJ: John Wiley & Sons.

DiMaggio, P.J., and W.W. Powell (1983). The iron cage revisited: Institutional isomorphism and collective rationality in organizational fields. *American Sociological Review*, 48(2), 147–160.

Grimaldi, J.V., and J. Trescott (2008a). West's travel tops other Smithsonian directors': Review found cost of trips by former Indian museum leader five times the average. *Washington Post*, February 2, C01.

———. (2008b). Ex-director to repay Smithsonian. Report criticizes spending by Indian Museum's West. *Washington Post*, October 29, C01.

Herman, R.D., and D.O. Renz (2000). Board practices of especially effective and less effective local nonprofits. *American Review of Public Administration*, 30(2), 146–160.

Hodge, M.M., and R.F. Piccolo (2005). Funding source, board involvement techniques, and financial vulnerability in nonprofit organizations: A test of resource dependence. *Nonprofit Management & Leadership*, 16(2), 171–190.

Hodgkin, C. (1993). Policy and paper clips: Rejecting the lure of the corporate model. *Nonprofit Management & Leadership*, 3(4), 415–428.

Inglis, S., and S. Cleave (2006). A scale to assess board members motivations in nonprofit organizations. *Nonprofit Management & Leadership*, 17(1), 83–101.

Jackson, P.M. (2006). *Nonprofit risk management & contingency planning. Done in a day strategies*. Hoboken, NJ: John Wiley & Sons, Inc.

Jeavons, T.H. (1992). When the management is the message: Relating values to management practice in nonprofit organizations. *Nonprofit Management & Leadership*, 2(4), 403–417.

Kovach, G.C. (2007). Oral Roberts U. and president part ways. *New York Times*, November 28. www.nytimes.com/2007/11/28/education/28roberts.html.

Meyer, J.W., and B. Rowan (1977). Institutionalized organizations: Formal structures as myth and ceremony. *American Journal of Sociology*, 83(2), 340–363.

Miller-Millesen, J.L. (2003). Understanding the behavior of nonprofit boards of directors: A theory-based approach. *Nonprofit and Voluntary Sector Quarterly*, 32(4), 521–547.

Ostrower, F. (2007). *Nonprofit governance in the United States: Findings on performance and accountability from the first national representative study*. Washington, DC: Urban Institute.

Powell, W.M., and P.J. DiMaggio (1983). The iron case revisited: Institutional isomorphism and collective rationality in organizational fields. *American Sociological Review*, 48, 147–160.

Silverman, L., and L. Taliento (2006). What business execs don't know—but should—about nonprofits. *Stanford Social Innovation Review*, 4(2), 37–43.

Stephens, J., and D.B. Ottaway (2003a). Nonprofit sells scenic acreage to allies at a loss: Buyers gain tax breaks with few curbs on and use. *Washington Post*, May 6, A01.

———. (2003b). Nature Conservancy suspends land sales. *Washington Post*, May 13. A03.

———. (2003c). Charity hiring lawyers to prevent probe. *Washington Post*, May 16. A27.

———. (2003d). 12 home loans at Conservancy. Nonprofit says all but 2 have been repaid; 5 came interest-free. *Washington Post*, June 13. A08.

———. (2005). Senators question Conservancy's practices. *Washington Post*, June 8. A03.

Strom, S., and J. Robbins (2008). Montana museum board breached duty, court says. *New York Times*, April 30. www.nytimes.com/2008/04/30/us/30museum.html.

Suderman, A. (2009). MontCo withholds money to charity because of high executive pay. *Washington Examiner*, May 12. www.washingtonexaminer.com/local/MontCo-withholds-money-to-charity-because-of-high-executive-pay-44840972.html.

Young, D. R. (2002). The influence of business on nonprofit organizations and the complexity of nonprofit accountability: Looking inside as well as outside. *American Review of Public Administration*, 32(1), 3–19.

# —————4—————

# Understanding Intergovernmental Relations and Public Policy

The Tampa Family Health Centers received more than $2.9 million, and the Suncoast Community Health Centers received $3.7 million to create jobs and improve medical services for Tampa Bay–area families. This was made possible because of the $2 billion made available to Community Health Centers through the American Recovery and Reinvestment Act (ARRA), passed on February 13, 2009.

ARRA provides spending and tax cuts aimed at stimulating the economy. Section 3(a) of the act, "Purposes and Principles," states that the "President and the heads of federal departments and agencies shall manage and expend the funds made available in this Act so as to achieve the purposes specified in subsection (a), including commencing expenditures and activities as quickly as possible consistent with prudent management" in order to:

- Preserve and create jobs and promote economic recovery;
- Assist those most impacted by the recession;
- Provide investments needed to increase economic efficiency by spurring technological advances in science and health;
- Invest in transportation, environmental protection, and other infra-structure that will provide long-term economic benefits; and
- Stabilize state and local government budgets, in order to minimize and avoid reductions in essential services and counterproductive state and local government increases.

Two hundred and fifty million dollars in federal grants have become available to health centers in medically underserved areas to build clinics and increase services at existing clinics for low-income patients such a homeless individuals, seasonal farm workers, and public housing residents who often can't pay for medical care. Health centers can apply for the grants through the Health Resources and Services Administration (HRSA). About 45 million people live in areas designated by the federal government as medically underserved (Fears 2010).

The nonprofit sector may also benefit by receiving other federal funds to provide programs and services through the federal agencies:

- The Community Development Institutions Fund (local economic growth in urban and rural low-income communities)
- Corporation for National and Community Service (VISTA, Ameri-Corps, Senior Corps, NCCC, Learn and Serve America)
- Department of Agriculture (nutrition assistance programs)
- Department of Education
  - State Fiscal Stabilization Fund (early-childhood education programs and elementary, secondary, and postsecondary education initiatives)
  - Title I (support programs for disadvantaged students)
  - Special Education
    * Impact Aid Construction (support construction activities for local education agencies that enroll federally connected children who receive funds under Section 8003 of the Impact Aid Program)
    * McKinney-Vento Homeless Assistance (address educational and related needs of homeless children and youth)
    * Independent Living Recovery Funds (provide support services for persons with significant disabilities, including Centers of Independent Living and OIB programs)
- Department of Energy (Energy Efficiency and Conservation Block Grant; Energy Efficiency Retrofits; energy conservation technologies, recycling, and other programs)
- Department of Health and Human Services
  - Adoption Assistance and Foster Care Program (support adoption and foster care programs)
  - Child Care Development Fund (support child-care services to working families or those looking for employment or receiving job training or education)
  - Community Health Centers (serve more patients, stimulate new jobs, and meet the demand for primary health-care services for uninsured or underserved populations)

- Community Services Block Grant (revitalize low-income communities and empower low-income families through programs that address poverty in urban and rural areas)
- Comparative Effectiveness Research Funding (to support health-care research)
- Immunization Grant Program (develop and sustain vaccination programs, increase the percentage of Americans who receive childhood vaccinations, and enhance public education and communication programs)
- Medicaid Relief (provide increased financial support for Medicaid programs)
- Senior Nutrition Programs (provide meals through community nutrition programs)
- Temporary Assistance for Needy Families (TANF) (provide emergency support for programs to provide services to families with children to transition from welfare to work by assisting with the development of vocation skills, employment placement, child-care services, and case assistance)
• Department of Homeland Security (allocations toward emergency food and shelter programs)
• Department of Housing and Urban Development
  - Public Housing Capital Fund (renovate public housing)
  - Native American Housing Block Grants (allocations for Native American housing programs for renovations and energy-efficiency modernization)
  - Assisted Housing Energy Retrofit (energy-efficient modernization and renovations)
  - Lead Hazard Reductions (assistance to lead-reduction programs)
  - Community Development Block Grants (funds to state and local governments for investment in community development programs that rehabilitate housing structures)
  - Homeless Prevention (funding programs that provide housing and vocational assistance)
• Department of the Interior (invest in water infrastructure, water recycling projects, environmental and ecosystem restoration, green buildings)
• Department of Justice (funds allocated to state and local law enforcement agencies and other criminal and juvenile justice programs)

- Department of Labor (allocations to the Workforce Investment Act (WIA) to provide grants to dislocated workers, adults, and youth)
  - Vocational Rehabilitation (assist individuals with disabilities prepare for, obtain, and maintain employment)
- National Endowment of the Arts (assist in funding arts projects and activities that preserve jobs in the nonprofit sector)
- National Science Foundation (assist in funding scientific research at universities and research facilities and provide financial assistance to graduate students pursuing careers in science)

Understanding intergovernmental relations is important for individuals affiliated with nonprofit agencies because the majority of national domestic programs are implemented through a complex arrangement among federal, state, and local governments. A government agency (at any level) can also establish agreements with organizations in both the nonprofit and private sectors to deliver goods and services deemed desirable and in the public interest. This chapter discusses the evolution in the relationships among the federal, state, and local governments and how those relationships affect public policies that in turn affect nonprofit organizations. As you read this chapter, reflect on the following questions and how understanding them can result in more proactive management strategies.

- How are nonprofits affected by public policies at the local, state, and federal level?
- Who are the relevant public policy makers at each level of government?
- How are nonprofits affected by funding relationships among the federal, state, and local levels of government?
- Why might there be a difference between what policy makers intend when they authorize government programs, and what happens when they are implemented?
- How are nonprofits affected by the indirect tools of government?

The relationship between the federal, state, and local governments has evolved over time and is linked to changes in American society. Initially, the United States operated on the belief that the functions and responsibilities of the federal and state governments were distinct—that the national and state governments were sovereign and equal within their respective spheres of authority as set forth in the U.S. Constitution. The national government exercised those powers specifically designated to it, and the remainders were reserved for the states (Tenth Amendment to the U.S. Constitution).

Federalism is a political system in which authority is divided between different levels of government. Power is divided between a central government and regional governments. In the United States, the U.S. Constitution divides power between the national and state governments. Federalism is a compromise between those who wanted a strong national government and those who preferred stronger state governments. Both the federal and state governments receive their authority to govern from the people. Powers of the federal government include conducting foreign relations, coining money, admitting new states to the union, declaring war, providing for national defense, regulating interstate commerce, establishing post offices, establishing courts inferior to the U.S. Supreme Court, and carrying out the powers implied by the necessary and proper clause of the U.S. Constitution. State powers include the authority to conduct elections and determine voter qualifications, establishing local governments, establishing a state militia, providing for public health, safety, and education, regulating intrastate commerce, and ratifying amendments to the federal Constitution.

Some powers referred to as concurrent powers are shared by both the federal and state governments. They include passing and enforcing laws affecting their residents, levying and collecting taxes, establishing court systems, borrowing and spending money for the general welfare, and chartering banks and corporations.

Because federalism tends to recognize mainly national–state relations and does not address the role of local governments, the term "intergovernmental relations" is more commonly used to describe the relationships between the federal, states and local governments. It is used to describe the complex and interdependent relationships among those at various levels of government as they seek to develop and implement public programs.

## Brief History

In the early days of the United States, there was limited intergovernmental funding. The earliest federal grants given to the states were land grants for the westward expansion. Congress awarded land grants because land was plentiful and money was not. Federal grants assisted in financing the construction of wagon roads, public schools, flood-control zones, agricultural experiments, and canals and waterways. In some instances the federal government awarded land grants to corporations building railroads. During this time the federal government played a very limited role in social services. On occasion it would assist states and local governments with social service projects that were beyond the resources of single localities. In 1817, Congress awarded a land grant to the Hartford Deaf and Dumb Asylum in Connecticut to educate deaf persons. The asylum, founded by Thomas Hopkins Gallaudet, was a joint effort by six New England states, as well as several churches. It was later renamed the American School for the Deaf, and it remains the country's oldest school for the hearing impaired (Kelly et al. 1983, 326–327). During the pre–Civil War era, proponents of states' rights and minimal national government prevailed. The post–Civil War era was one of weak government. Despite these conditions, the federal government did provide aid to states and localities on an ad hoc basis to address national disasters, civil disturbances, westward expansion, and the need for internal improvements. The Pacific Railroad Act of 1862 enabled the federal government to charter railroad corporations that constructed a transcontinental railroad, and the Morrill Act of 1862 provided land grants to establish land-grant universities (Canada 2003).

President Theodore Roosevelt believed that a strong executive branch was necessary to address the problems of the Industrial Revolution and reduce the division of governmental powers. The Weeks Act of 1911 authorized the secretary of agriculture to "cooperate with any state or group of states, when requested to, in the protection from fire of the forested watersheds of the navigable streams (P.L. 61–435; 37 Stat. 961). The act contained many mechanisms still in existence today that characterize the grant-in-aid system, such as requiring the approval of state plans, requiring matching state funds, and specifying the oversight role of federal officials (Grodzins 1966; Canada 2003). Within ten years of the passage of the Weeks Act, the federal government was awarding grants for highway construction, vocational education, public health, and maternity care (Canada 2003).

The Great Depression and the New Deal changed the relationship of the grants-in-aid system. There were new programs for social relief, financial reform, and economic recovery. State and local governments were unable to deal with the crisis. The national government cooperated with states and local governments to provide jobs and social welfare programs, develop the nation's infrastructure, and promote economic development. The Social Security Act of 1935 included national grants for state and local unemployment and welfare programs, and the Housing Act of 1937 involved the federal government in public housing. The Works Progress Administration (WPA) provided federal dollars and hired state-certified workers for locally initiated construction projects. The federal government also provided money for the arts and education. Federal programs operated through the states and local governments. As the number and amount of grants grew, the amount of federal control increased and the size of the federal government expanded. Federal, state, and local governments were interacting with one another in an attempt to resolve common problems. Some of the federal programs were centrally organized and administered, and workers were recruited and paid by Washington, DC. Others were locally initiated, designed, and financed by a combination of local grants and local dollars (Leighninger and Leighninger 2000).

The relationships among the federal, state, and local governments again changed as a result of Great Society programs proposed by President Lyndon B. Johnson. Programs were developed to assist low-income citizens. Improving and making health care more accessible, providing housing, legal services, employment and training programs, compensatory education programs, and community development programs were initiated. During this time the federal government became a more significant presence in the lives of state and local government administrators and in the delivery of government services to citizens. Calls for greater citizen and community participation meant that federal disbursements often went directly to cities and counties rather than through the states. The federal government moved into areas previously under state and local control—examples are Medicaid, the Elementary and Secondary Education Act (ESEA), the Model Cities Program, and the Economic Opportunity Act of 1964.

Government contracting for services expanded in the 1960s as a result of Great Society legislation such as the Economic Opportunity Act of 1964, 1967 amendments to the Social Security Act, the Model Cities Act, Community Development and Housing, the Neighborhood Youth Corps, Foster Grandparents, Medicare and Medicaid, the Older Americans Act, the Voting Rights Act, General Revenue Sharing, CETA, and Title XX of the 1974 amendments to the Social Security Act, allowing states flexibility while promoting fiscal responsibility. The above legislation encouraged the growth and availability of matching grants for the purchase of services by public agencies. Governments began contracting with nonprofit agencies for the delivery of social services. During the 1970s, social welfare became more privatized. Governments could contract for welfare services to be produced and delivered by private organizations whose donations qualified for part of the states' required local matching share of state grants (Gilbert 2000).

Federal assistance reaches nonprofit organizations indirectly through state and local governments that receive federal grants but retain substantial discretion in deciding whether to deliver the subsidized services themselves or to contract with nonprofit agencies or other public or private providers. The Social Services Block Grant, the Administration on Aging grant programs, alcohol, drug abuse, and mental health programs, and the Community Development Block Grant are examples of federal assistance that reaches nonprofits through this route (Salamon 1995).

This era of intergovernmental relations was characterized by joint planning and decision making at all levels of government, including partnerships with businesses and nonprofit organizations. Coalition building across the private sector, nonprofits, local governments, universities, poor people, and racial minorities was emphasized. More aid was aimed directly at local governments, school districts, and various nonprofit groups. Many of the new programs involved project grants, which required the grant recipients to search for matching funds and to meet planning and reporting requirements. In many cases, coordination among the various actors was often difficult, and to maintain control, the federal government issued categorical grants, which are federal funds provided for a specific purpose and restricted by detailed instructions, regulations, and compliance standards. Recipients of categorical grants lack discretion as to how the money should be spent.

The intergovernmental relations system became more difficult to manage. Federal administrators were required to oversee a larger number of separate programs, collaborate with more government units, and provide oversight for increasing amounts of money being transferred. Since grants often went directly to the agencies that ran federal programs, governors and mayors had less influence. As the number of grants-in-aid programs increased, there was a need for more professionals to administer them. As a result, program specialists at the federal, state, and local levels developed working relationships with each other that were often independent of the different legislative bodies and chief executives.

Because the program specialists shared a common policy or programmatic concern, they tended to interact more often with each other than with others at their same level of government but who were involved in other functional areas. For example, transportation, public health, or compensatory education became dominated by the relationships among professionals within various substantive areas of government rather than among elected officials and community members.

As public officials in Washington and the substantive policy experts at the state and local levels developed and directed policy, elected officials became more disconnected. They voiced concerns about losing influence over how local governments could spend national dollars. They also complained about categorical grants because their purposes were often narrowly defined, making it difficult for a state to adapt the federal grant to local needs. President Nixon heard their concerns and returned more autonomy to the states by distributing federal funds through block grants and general revenue sharing (which expired in 1986) rather than project or categorical grants.

*Block grants* are federal funds provided for a broad purpose, unrestricted by detailed requirements and regulations. State and local governments receive federal funds with little or no restrictions on how they might be used. This returned policy making, discretion, and responsibility to state and local governments and diminished Washington's policy control, resulting in greater autonomy and power for elected officials at the state and local levels. They could now determine how the federal funds were to be used.

The presidents that followed Nixon also wanted to reduce the size and scope of the federal government and create an intergovernmental relations system that gave more responsibility to state and local governments (most of them had been governors: Carter, Reagan, Clinton, and G. W. Bush). Many federal responsibilities and programs were devolved to the state and local levels (devolution is the transfer of power or authority from a central government to a state or local government). For example, the Omnibus Budget Act of 1981 changed the course of federal financial support to community mental health centers from direct funding to block grants where the states allocate the funds. The organization, structure, and funding of centers varies from state to state, as does the funding of mental health programs from state sources (Callicutt 2000).

The intent was to design a smaller, more efficient federal government with greater program and policy flexibility for the state and local governments. During this time, governments tended to enter into contracts for the purchase and delivery of services. Health and human services, public health, compensatory education, community development, and legal aid were just some of the services funded by public revenues and provided by individuals working for nonprofit organizations. During this time, nonprofits had become increasingly important in the delivery of public services. Lipsky and Smith noted that

> rather than depending mostly on private charity and volunteers, most nonprofit service organizations depend on government for over half of their revenues; for many small agencies, government support comprises their entire budget in contrast to the traditional relationship of two independent sectors; the new relationship between government and nonprofits amounts to one of mutual dependencies that is financial as well as technical. The line between public and private is blurred. (1989–90, 625)

Other scholars refer to this as "welfare pluralism," where there is a mixed economy of service providers: governments, nonprofits, and for-profits organizations all deliver social programs (Gilbert 2000).

This relationship continues to exist today. Therefore, nonprofit administrators must understand the complex intergovernmental environment if they are to manage effectively. While intergovernmental relations appear to complicate public policy and public programs, the result is a greater diversity in public policy and programs. States and local governments have different issues, and they may be better suited to deal with specific state and local problems.

## What Is Public Policy, and How Does It Affect Nonprofits?

A public policy is a general plan of action adopted by a government to solve a social problem, counter a threat, or pursue an objective. Public policy making is the combination of decisions, commitments, and actions made by those who hold government positions. Sometimes, government's plan of action is to do nothing, with the expectation that the problem will go away on its own, or in the belief that it is not or should not be government's business to solve it. Public policies are developed and carried out at the local, state, and national level, each with its own respective chief executive such as the president of the United States, the governor of a state, or a mayor. Chief executives influence policy by their appointment of department leaders and other officials. They can initiate legislation and determine policy directives. They can veto legislation passed by legislative bodies, as well as prepare budgets and issue executive orders.

Each level of government also has its own legislative body. At the national level it is the U.S. Congress. Each state has a state legislature, and local governments have city or county commissions, or township board of trustees. Legislative bodies appropriate funds, budgets are prepared by the executive staff, typically referred to as offices of budget and management, and final approval of the budget is made by legislative bodies. They initiate legislation, approve the executive appointment of department heads, provide oversight of government activities, conduct hearings, request audits of public programs, and initiate investigations into agency activities.

There is a federal court system composed of federal district courts, appellate courts, and the U.S. Supreme Court. States have their own court systems, as do larger local governments. Courts are involved in policy making through the interpretations they make. Vague legislation passed by legislative bodies allows for judicial interpretation. Laws passed by legislative bodies can be ruled unconstitutional, and courts have the authority to review decisions made by public agencies and to issue direct orders to agencies. Courts can overrule the actions of agencies, stop an agency from going beyond the intent of the legislation that created it, and issue injunctions that block an agency's actions.

Government administrative and regulatory agencies exist at each level of government. They are responsible for promulgating rules and regulations, providing oversight, and delivering services. The United States' federal system of government provides direction and regulates lower levels of government through federal mandates, transfers of money through federal grants, and regulation.

## Nongovernmental Actors in the Public Policy Process

Public policy is also influenced by a variety of other actors. In some states voters may become involved in policy making through their participation in local or statewide initiatives. *Initiatives* provide a means by which a petition signed by a certain minimum number of registered voters can force a public vote that decides the fate of a proposed statute, constitutional amendment, charter amendment, or ordinance. They differ from *referendums*, which are legislative acts that are referred for final approval to a popular vote by the electorate.

The news media influences public policy as well. What gets covered by newspapers, television, Internet sources, radio talk shows, and blogs can have an impact on public policy. Often these vehicles mobilize citizens to become politically active in regard to a particular issue.

Nonprofits, whether they are charitable nonprofits, social welfare nonprofits, chambers of commerce, labor unions, professional associations, or small nonprofits such as neighborhood groups and parent-teacher associations can also influence public policy. Nonprofits and their stakeholders are also affected by public policies. Nonprofits engage in advocacy, education, and lobbying activities, so it is important that they understand the public policy process. More on this topic will be discussed in chapter 8.

## The Public Policy Process

Many models have been developed over the years to describe the process of making public policy. A common model is a set of *policy processes*, which usually follow these five stages.

### *Problem Identification*

Policy problems need to be identified. Many problems confront Americans in their daily lives, but until they affect a greater number of people, government does not work to solve them all. When the government begins to consider acting on an issue, it has become part of the policy process.

### *Agenda Setting*

Agenda setting is the stage at which problems are defined as political issues and placed on the "set of issues" being considered at a particular point.

There is no single reason an existing social problem becomes redefined as a political problem. Sometimes, highly visible events or developments push issues onto the agenda. The rise in mortgage foreclosures called attention to the unregulated financial derivative markets. The 2005 hurricanes on the Gulf Coast region focused attention on poverty, flaws in the U.S emergency management system, growth management, zoning, and conservation issues (to identify just a few). And the 2010 *Deepwater*

*Horizon* oil spill in the Gulf of Mexico called attention to deepwater oil exploration and its long-term environmental impact as well as safety regulations on offshore drilling platforms. Issues may also reach the agenda through the efforts of scholars, think tanks, and activists urging more people to pay attention to a condition about which they may be unaware. Interest-group activities or actions by political leaders or public figures may increase the visibility of a situation. The publication of an influential book or public report can also call attention to an issue.

The likelihood that a certain problem will move onto the agenda is also affected by who controls the government and by broad ideological shifts. Agenda building also may involve redefining old issues so that people look at them in different ways, which is sometimes the result of interest-group complaints about a law's inadequacy or the lack of money allocated for protecting or advancing their concerns.

### Policy Formulation

Policy formulation is the creation of an action plan involving ways of solving a particular problem. Policy proposals can be developed by interest groups, executive staff, legislative bodies, state and local task force committees, civic associations, universities, advocacy groups, lobbyists, and think tanks. Policy formulation is the stage of the policy-making process in which formal policy proposals are developed and officials decide whether to adopt them. The most obvious kind of policy formulation is a proposal by the chief executive or the development of legislation by legislative bodies. Administrative agencies also formulate policy through the regulatory process. Courts formulate policy when their decisions establish new interpretations of the law. Policy is also formulated when the various participants in the policy process decide not to do anything.

Policy networks are the formal and informal relationships among interested parties that form agreements to achieve policy goals. Depending on the issue, such networks include members of Congress, state legislatures or local government councils and commissions, committee staffers, agency officials, lawyers, lobbyists, consultants, scholars, public relations experts, and other interest groups. Not all of the participants in the issue network have a positive working relationship with all of the others; at different times they may be allies or adversaries. What they have in common is expertise in a particular policy area. Policy becomes legitimized by the enactment of policies through the actions of elected officials, administrative agencies, or the local, state, and federal courts.

## Policy Implementation

Implementation is the execution of a policy. Policies become implemented through government expenditures allocated for the activities of public agencies and service providers. For federal policies, after a law is enacted and new regulations are written, individuals outside of Washington, DC, are typically responsible for implementing policy. They may be employees of nonprofits, for-profits, local governments, or state governments, or federal employees located in regional offices around the country.

## Policy Evaluation

Policy evaluation is the analysis of how well a policy is working. It tends to draw heavily on approaches such as cost-effectiveness analysis and statistical methods designed to provide quantitative measurements of program outcomes. Evaluation studies provide feedback about program performance. These studies can influence decisions about whether to continue, expand, alter, reduce, or eliminate programs.

## Policy Change or Termination

Changing or terminating policies often results after the analysis of a policy or program evaluation. Sometimes a shift in ideology results in a change or termination. Or issues that were once identified as problems may no longer be so, so the policy or programs developed to remedy the issue are discontinued. At other times, policies or programs may need to be adjusted. During the policy formulation and implementation stage, new issues or related problems may become evident, requiring that the policy be changed.

Nonprofits are affected by different types of public policies. Some of the more common types are regulatory, distributive, and redistributive policy.

1. *Regulatory Policy:* Limits the actions of individuals, groups, or corporations so as to protect the general public or a substantial

portion of the public. The enforcement of equal employment opportunity laws, occupational safety and health regulations, and environment protection are some examples.

2. *Distributive Policy:* Involves the allocation of benefits to certain segments of the population such as individuals, groups, and businesses, funded by the whole taxpayer base. Examples would be student loans and tax credits, mortgage-interest tax deductions, subsidies to farmers, and contracts for research and development activities.

3. *Redistributive Policy:* Involves the allocation of benefits or services to certain parts of the population by taxing others within the population to generate the funds. Income stabilization and health-care programs for the elderly or indigent are examples of redistributive policies.

## Additional Influences of Government

The federal government uses regulation, grant programs, and indirect government policies or programs to persuade state and local governments, individuals, nonprofits, and for-profit agencies to implement public policies it deems important (Kettl and Fesler 2009; Smith 2006; Salamon 2002).

### *Regulation*

Funding agencies can distribute money and require the recipients of money they distribute to be subject to certain conditions, such as complying with equal employment opportunity laws and affirmative action regulations, accounting for how the money is spent, conducting an environmental impact survey, and making projects accessible to disabled individuals. Programs also must abide by special rules. For example, Medicaid recipients must meet certain income guidelines.

### *Mandates*

Mandates are requirements that a high-level government imposes on a lower-level government, usually to perform some activity or provide a service. They are another form of administration through regulation. Unfunded mandates are specific rules and compliance obligations with no funding to implement them. Typically they are national policy goals that Congress has identified for all governments. They can consist of *direct orders*, which are requirements or restrictions enforced by one government upon another. *Crosscutting requirements* are mandates imposed on grant programs to achieve policy goals not central to a particular grant, such as environmental impact statements for construction projects or adherence to equal employment or affirmative action policies. *Crossover sanctions* are requirements imposed on one program to influence state or local policy in another. Failure to comply may lead the federal agency to reduce or cut off funds, even if the given program is administered properly. For example, the federal government required states to raise the age for purchasing and consuming alcohol to twenty-one or risk losing highway funds.

## *Grants*

Grants are a form of gifts that entail certain obligations on the part of the grantee and expectations on the part of the grantor. Grants are a means of providing states, local governments, nonprofits, for-profits, and individuals with funds to support projects the federal government considers useful.

*Categorical grants* provide money for a specific project with rules and compliance obligations on how the money can be used. Programs or projects funded by categorical grants are narrowly defined. To ensure compliance and uniform policy the legislation establishing a program and a grant is specific as to projects, eligible activities, rules and regulations reporting and auditing mechanisms.

Applicants for *project grants* are usually asked to justify the use they will make of the funds. There is no automatic entitlement to funds; the distribution of funds is determined by a federal administrator based on the application and review process.

Recipients of *formula grants* must meet criteria based on a legislated formula such as the income of the state's residents or its population, or the number of beneficiaries of a program who might benefit such as the elderly, poor, disabled, or youth. The formula grant is available to all applicants who meet the criteria. Typically, the recipient government is required to match a portion of the federal grant.

*Block grants* give money to state and local units for general purposes or broad functional areas instead of a specific project. The conditions to be met are less restrictive, giving greater flexibility and discretion to the grantee. These grants allow decentralized programmatic decision-making, giving local officials more influence on how funds will be spent. County governments may receive Social Services Title XX grants, but the range of services funded by Title XX can vary across states and county governments. Programs may be for child care or adult foster care, counseling, or adoptions. President Nixon consolidated 129 categorical grant programs into six block grants in education, law enforcement, community development, urban development, manpower training, and transportation. President Reagan, through the Omnibus Budget Reconciliation Act of 1981, combined 100 categorical grants into nine block grants: social services, low-income energy assistance, small-city community development, elementary and secondary education, alcohol and drug abuse, mental health, maternal and child care, preliminary health care, and preventive health. The intent was to reduce the size of the federal government and return the responsibility for programs to the states.

## Indirect Tools of Public Action

A great deal of public problem solving entails offering incentives to individuals or groups to engage in activities government supports. Salamon (2002) calls these indirect methods "tools of public action." Much of the growth of government activities over the last fifty years has taken place through the use of indirect tools or instruments. The political rationale is the desire to reduce the size of government agencies and programs. The instruments that are most important for nonprofit administrators to understand include the following.

### *The Use of Grants*

As noted above, grants are payments from a donor or government funder to a recipient organization to assist the agency in discharging its responsibilities. A grant is a gift to the recipient to "stimulate" or "support" some sort of service or activity, whether it be new or ongoing. Through grants, a grantor (government agency, foundation, funder) participates in the provision of a service while leaving to another entity (grantee) the task of actual performance. The responsibility for providing services is shared by multiple levels of government or governments, nonprofits, and for-profits.

## The Use of Vouchers

Vouchers are subsidies that provide an individual limited purchasing power to choose among a restricted set of goods and services. In a voucher system, the government subsidizes customers and permits them to exercise relatively free choice in the marketplace. For example, rather than subsidizing low-cost housing with grants or constructing additional housing, the government gives vouchers to eligible low-income individuals and families to apply toward rent at a home of their choice. Some states permit school vouchers allowing students to attend private schools. Federal Pell Grants for higher education are another example. The federal government provides the grants, but students select which institutions to attend. Vouchers are referred to as "consumer-side" subsidies rather than "producer-side subsidies" because the recipients decide where they go, rather than government directing them to certain services or providing direct expenditures to build more public housing.

There is some opposition to vouchers. Typically, they are limited to a maximum amount, so the voucher may pay for only a portion of the cost of service or benefit. Individuals with Section 8 vouchers may not be able to find housing that accepts the voucher, or the rents may still be too expensive. School vouchers may not cover the cost of tuition, and the private schools accepting vouchers may be located in areas that are far away from where the voucher recipients reside.

## The Use of Contracts

A *contract* is an agreement between government and a nonprofit or for-private firm to produce a good or service. It is a business arrangement between a government agency and a private entity that promises in exchange for money to deliver certain products or services to the government agency or to others on the government's behalf. Nonprofits providing public services are typically involved in the *purchase of service contracting (POS)*, in which the government contracts for the delivery of government-funded services by third parties to external recipients.

Governments may enter into different types of contracts. The most common are cost-reimbursement contracts, capitated or fixed-price contracts, and performance contracts. Under *cost-reimbursement contracts*, the government pays the contractor for all legitimate direct and indirect costs attributable to the contract. *Capitated* or *fixed-price contracts* pay the contractor a specific sum of money for well-defined products or services, usually for a fixed period of time. *Performance contracts* focus on the outputs and outcomes of service provisions and ties either contract payments, contract extensions, and renewals to their achievement.

Proponents of government contracting believe that market competition results in greater efficiency and that the provision of services may be less expensive because private organizations do not have to follow civil service rules and regulations. Because private agencies are subject to fewer public laws and less oversight than government agencies, they generally operate with greater flexibility. Often it is easier for a contractor to tailor a program to a given community. It may be less expensive for government to hire a private firm to deliver services than have a government agency hire more staff. Contracts can also be used to promote policies that government finds desirable, since the government contracts may require compliance in areas such as equal employment opportunity, paying a minimum salary, providing certain benefits, and maintaining a drug-free workplace.

Opponents of government contracting claim that important values such as responsiveness, fairness, transparency, accountability, and competence may become more problematic as the number of contract workers multiply (Kettl and Fesler 2009).

## The Use of Tax Expenditures

Government promotes activities it supports through favorable tax treatment. It pursues its objectives not by spending the tax dollars it collects, but by allowing individuals or corporations to keep and spend dollars they would otherwise owe the government. Government loses revenue because of tax law provisions that allow special exclusions, exemptions, or deductions from gross income, or that provide a special credit, preferential tax rate, or deferral of tax liability.

Tax deductions and tax credits are referred to as *tax expenditures*. These provisions in tax law encourage certain activities by individuals or corporations by deferring, reducing, or eliminating their tax obligation. A common example of a tax credit is the *dependent and child-care tax credit*, which allows parents to offset owed liability from their federal income tax. The cost of child-care (to a limited amount) can be deducted from the amount of taxes owed to the federal government. A common example of a tax deduction is the *home mortgage interest deduction*. This tax deduction offsets earned income. Homeowners can subtract the interest payments on their mortgages from their gross income when they complete their federal income tax forms.

## The Use of Loan Guarantees

Another indirect tool used by government is *loan guarantees*. These are loans guaranteed by the government to encourage a private lender such as a commercial bank or mortgage lender to offer loans to borrowers. The government enters into a contractual agreement to make full or partial payment to the lender if the borrower defaults on the guaranteed loan. The private lender originates the loan, secures the government guarantee, and services the loan according to government regulations or minimum standards. The intent behind loan guarantees is to encourage private lenders to offer loans to individuals with less than stellar credit histories.

## Tax-Exempt Bonds

Nonprofit hospitals, universities, housing development organizations, child welfare agencies, and mental health centers sometimes use tax-exempt bonds to finance the cost of capital improvements such as new construction or renovations.

These indirect instruments of public action permit the expansion of government activities without giving the impression that government has expanded. What does exist is a "shadow government" (Light 1999). Government is still financing the provision of services, but they are being provided by private agencies. Conservatives tend to believe in a limited role for government in social issues. They believe that help ought to come from family and voluntary or religious charities and not through government programs. Critics of this belief hold that the needs are too great, that many underrepresented and vulnerable citizens get lost in the policy process, and that private philanthropy does not provide enough resources (O'Connell 1999).

If government programs are desired, they should be organized and provided at the lowest level of government such as communities and states rather than the federal government. Peter Berg (1986, 1990) believes that local community-based agencies have the best chance of providing support. He refers to them as "mediating structures" because they mediate between those in need and governments to solve problems with local solutions and without a large federal bureaucracy.

## Conclusion

Public policy and intergovernmental relations affect nonprofits. They are regulated by the federal, state, and local governments. Nonprofit managers need to understand how public policies established at the different levels of government will affect their programs and services. In some cases, public policies may lead to the development or expansion of programs, as with the passage of the American Recovery and Reinvestment Act. And in other cases, public policies may lead to reduced funding and increased competition—for example, the increase in housing and school vouchers and increased contracting with for-private agencies to provide health and social services.

Many nonprofits receive a significant share of their funding from government grants and contracts distributed through a complex intergovernmental system. To be successful in managing and planning for the future, nonprofit managers must understand intergovernmental relations.

———————

### Case 4.1. Faith-Based Charities Are
### Hurting Due to Government Cutbacks

Faith-based social service organizations across the country are hurting from the dire economic times. As local, state, and the federal governments have cut back spending and reducing grants and contracts to social service providers, many agencies have had to lay off staff, eliminate programs, or try to borrow money in this tight lending market.

In a survey of fifty Catholic Charities affiliates nationwide, about 50 percent have experienced cutbacks or unpaid state contracts. In Illinois, a local Lutheran social services agency is owed $4 million. Another Lutheran social service agency in Minnesota closed four residential facilities for troubled adolescents, and in New Jersey, a cut of $1 million to Catholic Charities, which provided job training and other assistance to 400 mentally ill welfare recipients, forced it to eliminate the program and lay off around twelve staff. A cut of $300,000 by the state of California to the Jewish Family Service of Los Angeles required cutting seventy slots from a program that kept poor elderly people out of nursing homes by providing them with services in their homes.

*Source:* Salmon 2009.

———————

### Case 4.2. $50 Million for a Social Innovation Fund

Michelle Obama announced on May 5, 2009, that the administration planned to create a $50 million "social innovation fund" to help finance and expand promising nonprofit agencies.

The fund would provide support to nonprofit and community groups that focus on education, health care, economic mobility, and social issues. The administration plans to encourage foundations, philanthropists, and corporations to help raise additional money for the program.

> The idea is to find the most effective programs and provide them with the capital needed to replicate their success in communities around the country . . . by focusing on high-impact, results-oriented nonprofits, we will ensure that government dollars are spent in a way that is effective, accountable, and worthy of the public trust.

*Source:* Swarns 2009.

### APPENDIX 4.1.
### EXAMPLES OF PUBLIC POLICY MAKING

**Unintended Public Policy Implications: Nebraska's Safe Haven Law**

Legislators in the state of Nebraska passed a bill creating a safe haven to protect children. Parents could leave children at hospitals or police stations rather than neglect or hurt them. When the legislators passed the law, they were thinking of helpless children in immediate danger. Instead, many troubled adolescents were dropped off. One man dropped off nine of his ten children—his wife died the previous year, and he said he could not raise them alone. Other parents said their children were depressed or uncontrollable. Of the first thirty children abandoned in Nebraska, twenty-seven had received mental health services; twenty-eight came from single-parent households; and twenty-two had a parent or guardian who had been jailed. Parents from six other states left their children in Nebraska as well. The legislature fixed the law in a special session in November 2008.

*Source:* Searcey 2008; Slevin 2008.

## 660 New Laws Take Effect
## in Louisiana

In August 2010, 660 new state laws went into effect in Louisiana, only about two-thirds of the 1,063 laws adopted by the state legislature. The others will become law on specified dates or when the governor signs them. Two of the laws address abortion. One requires that a woman seeking an abortion have an ultrasound and be given a copy of the image, and the other one excludes doctors who perform elective abortions from participating in the state's medical malpractice coverage. One bill authorizes a church, synagogue, or mosque to allow some of its members to carry a concealed weapon as part of a security force during services. Police can stop a car if they see a driver seventeen or younger talking on a cell phone, texting, or using any electronic device. It is a crime to attend, bet on, or pay admission to a cockfight, punishable by a maximum $500 fine, up to six months in jail, or both. Historic landmarks and buildings, structures in historic downtown development districts, and arts and cultural districts are protected from graffiti-taggers.

*Source:* Anderson 2010.

## Local Policy Making:
## Nashville Won't Make English
## Its Official Language

In January 22, 2009, voters in Nashville, Tennessee, rejected a proposal to make English the city's official language. The proposal needed 50 percent of the votes to pass and received only 43 percent. If approved by the voters, it would have made Nashville the largest city to adopt the policy referred to as "English First." The proposal was opposed by a coalition that included the mayor of Nashville, civil rights groups, business leaders, ministers, and the leaders of nine colleges and universities.

*Source:* Brown 2009.

## Parents Protesting Cell Phone Towers Located on School Sites

In recent years, more than twelve schools in Hillsborough County, Florida, added cell towers to their campuses. In times of budget cutbacks, the principals were glad to receive the extra money for their schools from the cell towers, but parents have started organizing anti–cell tower campaigns. Some parents have threatened to stop fund-raising for the schools, while others talked about boycotting the Florida Comprehensive Assessment Test (FCAT) period. They are concerned about the health effects of exposing students to the towers.

*Source:* Stein 2009.

### Federal Statutory Law

The Lilly Ledbetter Fair Pay Act of 2009 is an act enacted by the 111th U.S. Congress and signed into law by President Barack Obama on Jan. 29, 2009. The bill amends the Civil Rights Act of 1964 by stating that the 180-day statute of limitations for filing an equal-pay lawsuit regarding pay discrimination resets with each new discriminatory paycheck. The law was a reaction to *Ledbetter v. Goodyear Tire & Rubber Co.,* 550 U.S. 618 (2007), a U.S. Supreme Court decision. The Supreme Court held that workers had only 180 days to file a pay discrimination lawsuit. Ms. Ledbetter was not aware of the pay discrepancy until the end of her nineteen-year career at Goodyear Tire and Rubber Company.

### *President Obama Issues Executive Orders*

In January 2009, President Obama signed an executive order requiring that the Guantanamo Bay detention facility be closed within a year.

EXECUTIVE ORDER—REVIEW AND DISPOSITION OF INDI-VIDUALS DETAINED AT THE GUANTÁNAMO BAY NAVAL BASE AND CLOSURE OF DETENTION FACILITIES

By the authority vested in me as President by the Constitution and the laws of the United States of America, in order to effect the appropriate disposition of individuals currently detained by the Department of Defense at the Guantánamo Bay Naval Base (Guantánamo) and promptly to close detention facilities at

Guantánamo, consistent with the national security and foreign policy interests of the United States and the interests of justice.

## U.S. Supreme Court Decision

In *United States v. Hayes,* the U.S. Supreme Court affirmed federal efforts to bar those convicted of crimes involving domestic violence from owning guns. In a 7–2 decision, Justice Ruth Bader Ginsburg said the law's intentions were clear: "Firearms and domestic strife are a potential deadly combination nationwide." No. 07–608. Argued November 10, 2008—Decided February 24, 2009.

## Rule Making

The Interior Department issued a regulation in December 2008 that took effect on January 9, 2009, allowing visitors to bring concealed, loaded guns into national parks and wildlife refuges. For more than twenty years they were allowed in those areas only if they were unloaded or stored and dismantled. Three nonprofit groups are seeking to overturn the rule: the Brady Campaign to Prevent Gun Violence, the National Parks Conservation Association, and the Coalition of National Park Service Retirees. Fish and Wildlife Service director Dale Hall and National Parks Service director Mary A. Bomar, both George W. Bush appointees, informed Congress shortly before the rule was finalized that they opposed allowing concealed weapons in refuges and parks. President Obama's appointee, Interior Secretary Ken Salazar, directed the National Park Service and the Fish and Wildlife Service to undertake a ninety-day review of any environmental considerations associated with implementation of the rules and to provide him with a report on the results of the review (Eilperin 2009). On May 12, 2009, in a 67–29 vote, the U.S. Senate voted to approve allowing loaded guns in federal parks. The measure was approved as an amendment to the bill that imposed new restrictions on credit card companies. President Obama signed the bill into law on May 22, 2009.

----

## References

Anderson, E. (2010). 660 new state laws take effect today. *New Orleans Times Picayune,* August 15. www.nola.com/politics/index.ssf/2010/08/660_new_state_laws_take_effect.html.
Berg, P.L. (1986). *The capitalist revolution: Fifty propositions about prosperity, equality, and liberty.* New York: Basic Books.
———, ed. (1990). *Capital spirit: Toward a religious ethic of wealth creation.* San Francisco: ICS Press.

Brown, R. (2009). Nashville won't make English official language. *New York Times,* January 23, A13. www.nytimes.com/2009/01/23/us/23english.html.

Callicutt, J. W. (2000). Social Policies and Mental health. In *The handbook of social policy,* ed. J. Midgley, M.B. Tracy, and M. Livermore, 257–276. Thousand Oaks, CA: Sage.

Canada, B. (2003). Federal grants to state and local governments: A brief history. Congressional Research Service Report RL30705. Washington, DC: Library of Congress.

Eilperin, J. (2009). Justice dept. defends Bush rule on guns. *Washington Post,* February 17, A03.

Fears, D. (2010). Health centers to get $250 million in grants to build clinics, boost services. *Washington Post,* August 18, A02.

Gilbert, N. (2000). Welfare pluralism and social policy. In *The handbook of social policy,* ed. J. Midgley, M.B. Tracy, and M. Livermore, 411–420. Thousand Oaks, CA: Sage.

Grodzins, M. (1966). *The American system.* Chicago: Rand McNally.

Kelly, A.H., W.A. Harbison, and H. Belz (1983). *The American constitution: Its origin and development.* 6th ed. New York: W.W. Norton.

Kettl, D.F., and J.W. Fesler (2009). *The politics of the administrative process.* 4th ed. Washington, DC: CQ Press.

Leighninger, L., and R. Leighninger (2000). Social policy of the New Deal. In *The handbook of social policy,* ed. J. Midgley, M.B. Tracy, and M. Livermore, 111–126. Thousand Oaks, CA: Sage.

Light, P.C. (1999). *The true size of government.* Washington, DC: Brookings Institution Press.

Lipsky, M., and Smith S.R. (1989–1990). Nonprofit organizations, government, and the welfare state. *Political Science Quarterly,* 104, 625–648.

O'Connell, B. (1999). *Civil society: The underpinnings of American democracy.* Hanover, NH: University Press of New England.

Salamon, L.M. (1995). *Partners in public service: Government-nonprofit relations in the modern welfare state.* Baltimore: Johns Hopkins Press.

———, ed. (2002). *The tools of government: A guide to the new governance.* New York: Oxford University Press.

Salmon, J.L. (2009). Government cutbacks leave faith-based services hurting. *Washington Post,* February 20, A01.

Searcey, D. (2008). Nebraska law leaves children in limbo. *Wall Street Journal,* November 12. http://online.wsj.com/article/SB122645008216719185.html.

Slevin, P. (2008). Nebraska to alter safe-haven law: State hopes to care for abandoned children without becoming a dumping ground. *Washington Post,* November 16, A03.

Smith, S.R. (2006). Government financing of nonprofit activity. In *Nonprofits and government: Collaboration and conflict,* ed. E.T. Boris and C.E. Steuerle, 219–256. Washington, DC: Urban Institute Press.

Stein, L. (2009). Amid discord over cell towers at schools, Hillsborough commissioners want halt in construction. *St. Petersburg Times,* February 11. www.tampabay.com/news/education/article974939.ece?comments=legacy.

Swarns, R.L. (2009). Mrs. Obama announces new fund to aid nonprofits. *New York Times,* May 6, A20. www.nytimes.com/2009/05/06/us/politics/06michelle.html.

# ——— 5 ———

# Where Revenues Come From and the Importance of Financial Management

Nonprofit agencies must anticipate and manage potential and actual changes in their revenues. Many health and human service nonprofits receive the majority of their revenue from government, whereas cultural institutions such as museums receive revenue from museum admissions, sales at gift shops, workshops or conferences, memberships, and fundraising events. Other nonprofits, such as social welfare and advocacy nonprofits, typically receive a significant share of their revenue from membership fees and donations. Despite the variety of independent-sector nonprofits in the United States, the context of nonprofit financial management has common characteristics that nonprofit leaders, employees, and board members need to understand, particularly the major streams of revenue and where they come from. Financial management involves a variety of concepts, principles, and tools designed to improve the use of resources to accomplish, in an efficient and effective manner, the mission, goals, and objectives of agencies and programs. Nonprofits need financial resources for long-term operating support as well as for stabilization and expansion (Martin 2001, 1).

As noted in the examples provided here and in earlier chapters, the environment that nonprofits find themselves in today is vastly different from a number of years ago when the economy was strong. Just a few years ago, due to the robust housing market, state and local governments were in strong financial shape and the stock market was thriving. Today, that no longer holds true. The federal government, state, and local governments have budget deficits resulting in laid-off and furloughed employees and reduced services, and they have less money available to give to nonprofits. Individuals, corporations, and foundations are also facing more difficult economic times and have cut back their donations and grants.

State governments have cut $55.7 billion from their budgets in the current fiscal year. Principal sources of revenue from personal income taxes, general sales taxes, corporate income taxes, and property taxes have continued to decline, leading some states to delay payments to nonprofits for services already provided to clients (National Conference of State Legislatures 2009; Surtel 2009; Timmons 2009; Winder 2009).

State governments are allowing for the incorporation of socially responsible but profit-motivated limited-liability corporations (L3Cs). There has been an increase in the number of for-private and nonprofit hybrid organizations competing with nonprofits for government and foundation contracts and grants.

The economic downturn has resulted in the elimination or the delay of capital improvements or the expansion of museums and performing arts centers (Pogrebin 2009).

An anonymous donor to the American Civil Liberties Union (ACLU) has withdrawn his annual gift of more than $20 million, leaving a 25 percent gap in its annual operating budget and forcing cutbacks in operations (Strom 2009).

More than ever, nonprofits need sound financial management. With so much distress in communities, there is even greater competition among health-care, education, housing, transportation, and infrastructure needs. If nonprofits fail to use their resources wisely, funders may decide not to renew funding or provide new contributions. Donors may also decide to contribute to different societal needs.

This chapter illustrates how financial management in the nonprofit sector can be more complex than in the private for-profit sector, due to the variety of revenue sources and because much of the revenue is restricted to spending on certain programs and services. As you read this chapter, reflect on how the following questions can result in improved financial management.

- How will reductions in government funding affect nonprofits?
- What are the risks in being dependent on only one revenue source?
- What strategies should be employed to diversify revenue sources?
- How does increased competition between for-profits and nonprofit hybrids affect nonprofit funding?

- Does the increased emphasis on social enterprise activities present challenges or opportunities for nonprofits?

## Where Do Nonprofit Revenues Come From?

If you were to ask most people where the lion's share of reporting public charity nonprofit revenue comes from, they would most likely respond donations. The reality is that in 2008, most sources were fees for services and goods from private sources (49.7 percent), followed by fees for services and goods from government (20.6 percent), private contributions (10.4 percent), investment income (6.9 percent), government grants (6.8 percent), and other income (5.5 percent). Fees from the sale of goods and services include patient care, including Medicare and Medicaid, tuition, or admission tickets (Wing, Roeger, and Pollak 2010).

An explanation of the different types of revenue follows.

### Fees for Services and Goods

Nonprofit fees are associated with services or goods. They might be university or day-care tuition or ticket sales. Membership dues or assessments are payments that organizations receive in exchange for membership privileges.

### Private Contributions

Donations and gifts are voluntary charitable gifts of money, goods, equipment, services, and property. Donors can place restrictions on how a nonprofit may use gifts or contributions. Some donations or gifts are made to the general fund and are unrestricted, while others are made with conditions as to how they may be used. Gifts and contributions can be cash or other assets given to a nonprofit to support its exempt activities. Donors may be corporations, foundations, or individuals, who may also designate bequests. Funds obtained through general fund-raising activities and special fund-raising events are considered to be private contributions. Nonprofits also accept nonmonetary contributions such as volunteer services; materials and supplies; the use of factory, automotive, and office equipment; factory or office space in a building; the use of intangible assets such as patents or copyrights; advertising time or space; and similar goods or services.

## Investments Income

Some nonprofits make investments in securities. They are generally allowed to engage in the same sorts of investment transactions as for-profit entities, as well as benefit from interest income on short-term investments such as savings accounts.

## Other Income

Unrelated business income is from a trade or business that is regularly carried on by an exempt organization and that is not *substantially related* to the performance by the organization of its exempt purpose or function. Nonprofits may sell literature and other materials to members, the public at large, other nonprofits, and others. Nonprofits receive income by renting out equipment or space. Under certain circumstances, some types of nonprofits, such as performing arts organizations, make facilities available to concessionaires who provide goods on a commercial basis. Auxiliary activities, another source of income for nonprofits are undertaken for the benefit of their employees, members, or public clientele but are not the primary activities for which the nonprofit was organized. For example, a nonprofit might run a cafeteria for the convenience of its employees.

## Contracts and Grants

Some grants are unrestricted and are given to enable nonprofits to get started by having the resources to build and support the organization. Other grants and contracts are awards for performing a specific service. Grants are typically governed by agreements or contracts specifying what the recipient organization must do in return for the funding. Typical conditions include restrictions on how the resources are used; requirements that agencies comply with specific laws, regulations, and practices in a wide range of areas; and measurable goals and service requirements, such as specific results or levels of goods or services to particular groups of individuals.

Grant agreements may also define the eligibility standards for the groups or individuals to be served; additional funds or other resources that must be provided as a matching share; allowed and unallowed expenditures; procedures for making changes in the specific amounts, categories, or line items contained in an approved budget; and specific hiring, personnel, accounting, cash management, record-keeping, reporting, and auditing requirements.

Some grantors may require that the nonprofit provide a *matching grant,* usually defined as a percentage of the resources the nonprofit needs to operate the specific program or activity. It may be a cash match, or an in-kind match such as contributions of rental space, equipment, materials, or services, as long as the fair market value of the in-kind goods or services equals the required matching amount. Some grants may require a combined cash and in-kind match.

*Challenge grants* have special program matching requirements, whereby a funding source promises to give funds to a nonprofit once it has attracted a specific amount of new support from other outside sources.

*Government grants* may require all of the above as well as other provisions. Nonprofits that receive federal, state, or local government funds may be subject to auditing requirements in addition to Generally Accepted Auditing Standards (GAAS). The General Accounting Office's Government Auditing Standards, known as the Yellow Book, set additional audit requirements; the Office of Management and Budget Circular A-133: Audits of States, Local Governments and Nonprofit Organizations has its own requirements; and nonprofits may have to comply with applicable state, city, or other local government audit requirements as well.

*Foundation grants* can be important sources of contributions that warrant tracking them separately from other contributions.

## Restricted and Unrestricted Funds

The types of income and the manner in which they are received will affect virtually every aspect of a nonprofit organization's financial management system (Dropkin and Hayden 2001). Support should be diversified, so the organization is not overly influenced by one source of funding and subject to the risk that would result if that source declines.

Unrestricted net assets are "neither permanently restricted nor temporarily restricted by donor-imposed stipulations." Temporarily restricted net assets are limited to specific purposes or time periods specified in contracts, grant agreements, or other written or oral statements. Permanently restricted assets such as endowments are held in perpetuity for a specific purpose, although the nonprofit can classify income generated from the principal amount as temporarily restricted or unrestricted, depending on donor stipulations. These donor restrictions on the use of net assets may be conveyed either orally or in writing and may be made at the time the resources are given.

Contributions that are not specifically designated as temporarily or permanently restricted will be considered unrestricted. Funds provided by government agencies are more likely to have specific performance requirements than those provided by private individuals or foundations, whereas, funds acquired through special events and general fund-raising activities are typically unrestricted.

## The Importance of Government Money

Public finance at all levels of government affects nonprofit organizations. Some nonprofit agencies may be heavily dependent on government funding. Health and human service nonprofits typically rely on government contracts and grants for most of their funding, whereas cultural institutions, still the recipient of some government funds, also rely on earned income, fees for services, and donations.

### *Federal Government*

The major source of revenue for the federal government is the personal income tax levied on U.S. residents. This tax provides somewhat less than half of federal revenues and has remained fairly consistent as a share of revenues over time. Payroll taxes are the second-largest source of federal revenue. They are deducted out of each paycheck and fund social insurance programs such as Social Security, Medicare, and unemployment insurance. Many Americans do not realize that corporate tax revenues provide less than 14 percent of federal revenue. Excise taxes levied on the consumption of certain goods such as tobacco, alcohol, and gasoline also contribute some revenue to the federal government.

The largest single program that the federal government spends money on is Social Security. Other entitlement programs such as Medicare, Medicaid, and welfare programs make up approximately 30 percent of spending. Approximately half of all federal spending goes to programs that require automatic spending if individuals meet eligibility criteria. Entitlement programs in the United States such as Social Security and Medicare affect nonprofits. Those programs are indexed to cost-of-living increases, meaning that their benefits rise with inflation. Two-thirds of the federal budget is for uncontrollable expenditures; the remainder is for discretionary spending. Almost two-thirds of the federal budget is made up of mandatory spending, without elected officials having the discretion to determine where the money goes. Spending on interest on the national debt and other mandatory obligations means that budget choices are made for only a third of federal spending.

## *State and Local Governments*

At the state and local levels, there is greater variation, but the major sources of revenue are sales taxes, including state and local excise taxes on products such as cigarettes and gasoline; federal grants-in-aid; the redistribution of funds from the federal government; income taxes, and property. State spending is typically centered on education, Medicaid and welfare programs, social services, transportation, corrections, and property tax credits. Some states, such as Florida, do not have a state income tax so are they more reliant on property, sales and excise taxes, and the state lottery to fund public education.

For local governments, there is even greater variation. Local governments are heavily dependent on the property tax and state transfers of funds. Local governments also collect revenue through user charges such as fees for garbage collection and recreation programs. They may also impose an additional sales tax, and in some communities, local governments impose income or residency taxes. Most of local government spending goes to police and fire services, public education, public health and social services, transportation, and sewer and water services. Other local government spending is for parks, libraries, and cultural institutions.

Government spending reflects the priorities of taxpayers and politically active constituents. Elected officials and public administrators attempt to meet the demands of their constituents' different preferences. Decisions have to be made as to what gets funded. Public budgets reflect public policy and the commitment toward achieving certain goals for the nation. This is why nonprofits need to understand how public policies are made and implemented, along with the regulations governing lobbying, and be vigilant advocates for their programs and services. Decreases in public revenues affect not only direct government services and programs but also nonprofit services and programs.

## Developing a Budget and Tracking the Money

On the governance and policy level, the board of directors should be concerned with what programs will be undertaken in keeping with the organization's mission, how much of the organization's resources will be allocated to each program, and what will be the sources of funds for financing each program. The support and the nature of the programs have implications beyond the budget because they affect the tax-exempt status of the nonprofit.

A budget is a projection of costs and revenues that is approved by the board of directors. It is the financial plan for implementing the mission of the nonprofit. It identifies where its revenues are coming from to pay for the services and programs it plans to deliver in the upcoming year. Before programs can be implemented, a budget must be adopted so that the managers know the amount of resources planned for their programs, the sources of those dollars (grants, fees, fund-raising efforts), how those dollars are expected to be allocated among competing uses within each program, and a schedule of expenditures and receipts over the life of the program.

Actual spending and receipts can be tracked against planned targets. Variances between actual and budgeted performance signal the need to slow spending or increase receipts, or to shift resources from one category to another, or to raise more funds. Although it is not audited, the budget may be used by auditors to judge the extent to which the nonprofit exercises foresight and control over its spending and revenues. Any variances between actual and planned expenditures or receipts indicate the nonprofit may be off course and should get the attention of management.

In nonprofit accounting, like public accounting, resources in accounts are in different funds; each fund has its own set of accounts and is considered to be a separate entity. The purpose is to ensure that the nonprofit uses the resources made available to each fund only for the purposes designated by that fund.

Resources are typically limited, so nonprofits have to decide how to distribute the funds it expects to have. Developing a budget requires nonprofits to determine their limits. They must identify the sources of funds and how they will be used. A nonprofit may structure its allocations on the basis of units or departments, programs, activities, or managers. In some cases, particular resources will be tied to particular units or programs, as in grants or restricted gifts. The budget process must distinguish those funds that are earmarked for specific purposes and then distribute the unrestricted funds at its disposal. In many cases, it will consider some programs to more or less stand on their own because of earmarked funds or their ability to bring in new resources, and other programs will be identified as most in need of resources.

Many funders have shifted from cost-reimbursement contracts, where nonprofits were reimbursed for their actual expenses, to performance contracts, where nonprofits are paid a fixed fee per output or unit of service provided or per client outcome achieved. Performance contracts place greater financial responsibility for performance on nonprofits. Unless there exist accurate cost data, including overhead costs and rates, nonprofits may underprice their services and lose money on contracts. As a result, nonprofits are required to understand performance budgeting, program budgeting, cost analysis, the determination of overhead rates, and the pricing of agency services (Martin 2001).

There has also been a shift to funding programs and not agencies. The Government Accounting Standards Board (GASB) in its service efforts and accomplishments (SEA) reporting initiative makes programs its basic unit of analysis. A program is defined as a major ongoing activity or service with its own set of goals, objectives, policies, and budgets that produces a defined product or service (Martin 2001, 11). Small nonprofits may have only one program, whereas larger nonprofits often have many. Programmatic responsibilities and financial management responsibilities should be developed and evaluated together. To emphasize the relationship between programs and their costs, some nonprofits have organized their programs into *responsibility centers* to address financial accountability. There are different types of responsibility centers concerned with different types of financial accountability. A program can be designated as an *expense center,* a *revenue center,* a *profit center,* an *investment center*, or any combination.

In an *expense center*, programs and program managers are responsible for managing their own expenses. Budgets are developed for each individual program. Once budgets are developed, it becomes the responsibility of the program managers to oversee, monitor, and approve program expenses in order to ensure that budgets are not exceeded.

In a *revenue center*, programs and program managers are responsible for helping to generate either a portion, or all, of the revenue necessary to cover program expenses. Program managers cannot depend on others for revenues. They have to be assertive in developing and submitting grant proposals, respond to request for proposals (RFPs), and determine fees and donation polices. Program managers need to monitor their revenue streams on a monthly basis and take steps to identify new revenue sources. They must also strive to control and reduce expenses. Program managers are asked to assist the larger agency in generating sufficient revenues to fund their programs.

In *profit centers*, program managers are held accountable for generating revenues in excess of expenses (earning a profit). For example, a multipurpose mental health center might have both paying clients and those that pay on a sliding scale who receive services as part of a government grant or contract. The service price charged to full-pay patients is at market rates and covers the cost of care plus a little extra. The excess revenues over expenses (profit) are then used to offset the costs of providing care to sliding-scale clients or the government contract.

*Investment centers* exist to manage endowments, investments, and the other assets of a nonprofit. Whether or not a nonprofit has an investment center depends on its size and wealth. Small nonprofits are not likely to need an investment center, but larger nonprofits like hospitals or museums may. Some programs can have multiple responsibilities and center designations.

A budget should not be prepared until the nonprofit's policies, priorities, and plans have been clarified. The budget must be approved by the board of directors in a manner that involves questioning and analysis. The approval of the budget should be regarded as a commitment to carry out the policies, respect the priorities, and support the plans included in the budget.

For nonprofits that operate several different programs, endowments, or businesses, the organization's final budget may be a composite of several sub-budgets, such as one for each activity within each program or functional area, one for each program or functional area, and one for the organization as a whole, which is a composite of all functional or program areas plus general administration.

Gulf Coast Jewish Family Services Inc. & Gulf Coast Community Care Division is located in the city of Clearwater, Florida, but provides a variety of services across the state. It runs ten programs and services for Jewish families that are supported in part by the Jewish Federation of Pinellas/Pasco Counties. It also provides twelve different mental health services, seven different children and family services, five different employment programs, five programs for the elderly and people with a disability or HIV, two different refugee service programs, and four different affordable-housing programs. Its balance sheet for 2007–2008 was $12,788,316 net assets (Gulf Coast Jewish Family Services Inc.

& Gulf Coast Community Care Division 2008). Its funders include a combination of federal, state, and local government funding, federated foundations, family foundations, and United Way agencies:

Agency for Health Care Administration
Agency for Persons with Disabilities
Alliance for Human Services
Area Agency on Aging of Pasco-Pinellas
Area Agency on Aging of West Central Florida
Central Florida Behavioral Health Network
Children's Board of Hillsborough County
Children's Services Council of Brevard County
City of Clearwater
City of Largo
City of St. Petersburg
City of Tampa
Coalition for the Homeless of Pasco County
Conference on Material Claims Against Germany
Emergency Food and Shelter Program
Florida Attorney General
Florida Department of Children and Families
Florida Department of Corrections
Florida Department of Education
Florida Department of Elder Affairs
Florida Department of Financial Services
Florida Department of Transportation
Gelbart Foundation
Glazer Family Foundation

Heartland for Children
Hillsborough County Health & Human Services
Hillsborough County CDBG Community Development Block Grant
Hillsborough County Criminal Justice
Hillsborough KIDS Inc.
International Commission of Holocaust Era Insurance Claims
Jewish Federation of Pinellas County
Lee County
Mazon: A Jewish Response to Hunger
Ounce of Prevention Fund
Pasco County
Pinellas County Community Development Block Grant (CDBG)
Pinellas County Health & Human Services
Pinellas Substance Advisory Board
Rothman Family Foundation
Sarasota Family YMCA
Schoenbaum Foundation
South Florida Workforce Board
United Nations Voluntary Fund for Victims of Torture
U.S. Department of Housing & Urban Development
U.S. Office of Refugee Resettlement
United Way of Pasco County
United Way of Tampa Bay
WorkNet Pinellas

## Social Enterprise, Nonprofit Hybrids, Nonprofit Ventures

The present economy has focused immediate concerns on the sustainability of most nonprofits. As the earlier chapters indicate, nonprofits are folding, merging, reducing their workforces, and reducing or eliminating programs. However, there have been concerns about the effectiveness of traditional approaches to meeting social needs. For longer than the past decade, there has been an emphasis on searching for innovative solutions to financing and managing nonprofit organizations (Brinckerhoff 1996). Some nonprofits such as large performing arts centers have followed business models for setting ticket prices and marketing their programs and performances. Nonprofits in the social sector have also moved to some market-based approaches, shifting away from a heavy reliance on philanthropy and government funding and adopting different approaches to address funding needs (Brinckerhoff 1996, 2000a, 2000b; Dees 1998; Dees et al. 2001, 2002).

The market-based approaches are often referred to as social enterprise, nonprofit ventures, and nonprofit hybrids (Brinckerhoff 1996, 2000a, 2000b; Dees 1998; Dees et al., 2001, 2002; Kirlin 2006). Instead of relying on private grants or government assistance, these organizations are conceived as self-supporting operations that generate fees and commercial revenues to support their charitable missions or generate earned income to serve a social mission.

Some of the activities that have been undertaken include exploring commercial methods of generating revenues, starting mission-related businesses, and forming mutually beneficial partnerships with corporations (Dees 1998; Austin et al. 2006). In the United States, social enterprise falls along a continuum from profit-oriented businesses engaged in socially beneficial activities such as corporate philanthropies or social responsibility to businesses that include profit goals with social objectives (often referred to as hybrids), to nonprofit organizations engaged in commercial activities to support their missions (Cordes and Steuerle 2009; Dees 1998; Kirlin 2006). Current research often focuses on the "double bottom line" whereby a nonprofit is organized to create economic value through a commercial bottom line, defined in terms of market revenue and cost, and a social bottom line that identifies and values mission-related outputs that have social value not explicitly captured in the marketplace (Cordes and Steuerle 2009, 3). Low-profit limited liability corporations (L3Cs) and B corporations noted in chapter 1 are examples.

These initiatives can take the form of for-profits, nonprofits, or government programs, and they exhibit three characteristics:

1. *Social innovation*, which includes finding, testing, and honing new and potentially transformative ways of approaching social problems;
2. *Accountability* through measuring results, continuously making improvements based on those results, and sharing performance and outcome data with stakeholders;
3. *Sustainability*, which includes identifying reliable financial and other types of support by utilizing markets, forming partnerships across sectors, and responding to stakeholder needs to ensure that the solution will be enduring (Wolk 2008).

For nonprofits, commercial activity may include only revenues that support other programs or services offered by the nonprofit, or activities that generate revenue as well as provide programs that are consistent with their mission goals, such as sheltered workshops for the disabled or educational programs at an aquarium or zoo. Social enterprise that nonprofits engage in may take a number of different organizational forms, including internal commercial ventures, for-profit and nonprofit subsidiaries, and partnerships with business such as cause-related marketing (Dees 1998; Kirlin 2006). Young (2009) provides this general definition to capture the variety of social enterprise activities: "social enterprise is activity intended to address social goals through the operation of private organizations in the marketplace" (23).

## Proceed with Caution

Many nonprofits were thrust into market-based activities without undergoing a careful analysis to see if they would be beneficial. While conceptually the idea and promise of social enterprise activities are attractive, there are challenges that must be recognized. Some of the identified challenges for nonprofits include the difficulty of building new organizational capacities and the lack of the staff or infrastructure needed to successfully pursue enterprise activities. Clashes among employees, donors, board members, and programs that already exist may result from a different emphasis on funding. Individuals and funders may reduce their contributions if they disagree with the change in direction or if they think that the nonprofit is now less reliant on donations. To key stakeholders, it may appear that nonprofits are drifting away from their mission. There is also the risk of failure. The failure rate for for-profit organizations is extremely high (Oster et al. 2004). If businesses developed to make a profit and to target a particular audience, customer, or client often fail, then why do nonprofits think that they can make a profit? Young (2005) provides an excellent explanation of the mission-market tension in managing nonprofit agencies.

The largest percentage of nonprofits are in the health and human services field, and they address the problems of society's most vulnerable citizens. Providing services to those who are sick, homeless, in need of social support, rehabilitative services, increased education, or job training is expensive. One has to recognize that market-based strategies will not work for all nonprofits.

While nonprofits have an obligation to be managed effectively and efficiently, it must be recognized that not all nonprofits will be able to generate revenues, given the clientele they serve and the types of services they provide. Sometimes nonprofits have rushed to enter for-profit ventures without first understanding the strength of proposed endeavors. Seedco, a nonprofit that runs workforce development and small-business support programs, launched a program to provide emergency child care to low-income workers so they would not have to miss work when their primary care fell through. It was set up as a social enterprise titled Community Childcare Assistance (CCA). Seedco contracted with child-care providers, and then sold the program to businesses as an employee benefit. Seedco thought the program would cover much of its budget, help working parents keep their jobs, ensure quality care for their children, and give business to small child-care centers. But few employers joined the program, in part because it could not accommodate sick children or late shifts. Seedco discontinued the program, noting that the program was too complex for an organization without experience in either business or child care. In a follow-up analysis of its social enterprise experience, Seedco's Policy Center found that nonprofits driven to meet "a double bottom line for customers and clients have far more typically led to frustration and failure, drawing attention and resources from the organization's core work—and that even the oft-cited success stories are less cut-and-dried than they appear" (2007, 2). Seedco's analysis could not identify a single example of an entirely self-sustaining nonprofit-based social enterprise. What they found were nonprofits that use a combination of overt and hidden government and foundation subsidies that allow them to pursue their social goals while remaining competitive.

One Plus: One Parent Families, the largest social enterprise in the United Kingdom, needed to discontinue its operation when it was no longer financially viable. Higgins and Finnie (2010) provide a case study of the lessons learned in its failure, shutdown, and transfer of services.

Conducting a review of the profitability of social enterprise ventures, Foster and Bradach (2005) found in a random sample of ventures in 2001 that 71 percent lost money, 5 percent broke even, and 24 percent turned a profit. They note that even those claiming success probably undercounted indirect costs such as managerial time from the nonprofit or unaccounted subsidies for startup costs. They provide an example of a nonprofit that developed and sold MYS Salad Dressing. The nonprofit thought it was producing a bottle of salad dressing for $3.15 and could sell it for $3.50, collecting a 35 cents profit on each bottle. But when all of the direct and indirect costs were accounted for, the salad dressing actually cost $10.33 per bottle.

It is important to note that there are successful social enterprise efforts, such as DC Central Kitchen, which offers a culinary training program for homeless individuals while also operating social enterprises such as selling frozen meals to grocery stores, offering catering services, and selling food from street carts. Some affiliates of Habitat for Humanity have added additional services like ReStore retail outlets, demolition of distressed properties, and home repair microfinancing. The Crisis Center of Tampa Bay operates a social enterprise called TransCare that provides 911 Basic Life Support services in the city of Tampa and Hillsborough County, countywide psychiatric transports to and from area hospitals, transportation to state psychiatric facilities, and stretcher service and stand-by service for special events (Crisis Center of Tampa Bay 2010).

Dees (2004), in putting nonprofit business ventures in perspective, notes that many nonprofits look at business ventures to diversify their revenue streams, but they miss the point that if the incremental revenues do not exceed the incremental costs of running the venture, the venture will be a net drain on the parent organizations. They will have to raise more money to subsidize the venture, possibly at the expense of mission-oriented programs. It is also important to note that the implementation of services and products is more difficult than developing a business plan (Caesar and Baker 2004, 207). Austin et al. (2006) identify important differences in entrepreneurship between the commercial and social sectors. They are market failure, mission, resource mobilization, and performance measurement in business and social sectors. *Market failure* is attributed to commercial market forces not meeting a need such as in public goods or contract failure. Often the recipients of nonprofit services are unable to pay for them. *Mission* recognizes that the fundamental purpose of social entrepreneurship is creating social value for the public good, whereas commercial entrepreneurship aims to create profitable operations resulting in private gain. This variation can affect the motivation of personnel and management activities. The commercial and social dimensions within an agency may be a source of tension. *Resource mobilization* recognizes that the no-distributive restriction on revenue surplus generated by nonprofits and the social purposes of for-profit and hybrid forms of social enterprise limit access to the same capital markets that commercial entrepreneurs have. Raising money for activities may be more difficult for nonprofits. *Performance measurement* is easier for commercial enterprises than for social enterprises. For-profit enterprises can rely on tangible and quantifiable performance measures such as financial indicators, market share, and customer satisfaction. Social enterprises are accountable to a greater number of stakeholders and have greater difficulty in measuring social change. The relationship between stakeholders and assessing of performance is more difficult in nonprofits than in for-profits.

This is not to suggest that social enterprise activities not be undertaken—there have been many successful social enterprise endeavors—only that rigorous research be undertaken in advance. All nonprofits should clarify their goals, review internal procedures, project revenues, and develop a sound fiscal plan, as well as be vigilant in looking for ways to improve services and programs.

## Conclusion

The uncertain external environment requires that nonprofit administrators, boards of directors, and program staff members manage financial resources effectively. They need to stay abreast of current events and changes in funding opportunities, and develop internal controls to promote accountability. Many nonprofits rely on multiple funders that may have conflicting demands and reporting requirements. Fund-raising may be difficult when the economy is suffering and service demands increase. In the pursuit of diversifying their funding, nonprofits may find themselves spread too thin. Declines in grants and contracts from foundations and the public sector, along with a decline in individual and corporate donations, have placed many nonprofits in weakened financial positions. Because of the success of some nonprofit social enterprise ventures and hybrid agencies, many nonprofits have been encouraged by their board of directors, foundations, and management assistance agencies to pursue social enterprise activities. Recognizing the importance of diversifying sources of income is important; however, nonprofits must exercise caution and undertake comprehensive research and fact-finding before beginning enterprise activities. There have been some noted successes—for example, the Joffrey Ballet began to offer dance classes to generate income to offset budget reductions due to a decline in ticket sales and corporate donations. The classes are taught in the group's existing space, by Joffrey's dancers, and the ballet's staff handles marketing, so there are no substantial expenses. Some rehabilitation facilities and nursing homes have begun to sell meals and offer fitness classes to the community, while others operate pain management clinics. Others believe that it would be more effective to make changes in tax policy that assist nonprofits by encouraging individuals, foundations, and corporations to increase their donations to them than to encourage nonprofits to pursue for-profit ventures (Foster and Bradach 2005; Weisbrod 2004).

---

### Case 5.1. Goodwill Superstore to Sell 80,000 New and Used Products

In Oldsmar, Florida, a new Goodwill superstore opened in 2009. It has 25,000 square feet, which is the size of a typical Barnes & Noble, and it sells 80,000 new and used products.

"Successful stores are critical to Goodwill's mission, as retail revenue helps support the agency's human services. The agency's retail operations are also closely integrated with Goodwill's training programs for people with developmental disabilities, creating opportunities for paychecks and empowerment," according to a Goodwill spokesperson.

The cost of building the store was $3.6 million, and projected revenues for the first year are $2.5 million. When asked why Goodwill invested in a superstore during tough times, the spokesperson responded, "The customer base has increased in this economy, rather than contracted. . . . Donations are down somewhat, but we are hopeful that the residents of North Pinellas will find it convenient to drop things off at the store's drive through and help make a difference in people's lives. We are a very large nonprofit with good financial management. The superstore business is financially sound, based on our first superstores built in 2001–2002. Plus, the expansion plans were made several years ago, and the multistore project began in 2007, so we were committed to it."

*Source:* Schulte 2009.

---

### Case 5.2. Cause-Related Marketing or Consumption Philanthropy?

Most of us have seen products supporting pink ribbons and Product Red products such as red laptop computers, t-shirts, and iPods that, when purchased, result in a percentage of the sale price going to support non-profits. We have also seen the logo from the American Heart Association on consumer products as an endorsement that the product is heart healthy. There are different types of relationships among nonprofits and corporations. Eikenberry (2009) describes three:

1. *Transactional* is the most common. For each unit or service a corporation sells, it contributes a portion of the proceeds to a social cause; for example, pink products contribute to the Susan G. Komen For the Cure Breast Cancer Foundation.
2. *Promotion*-based, by which a corporation promotes a charitable cause and makes a contribution to it. The donations are not necessarily tied to a business transaction and are not necessarily monetary, but they do promote the cause and the corporation. An example is the partnership between the Anti-Defamation League and Barnes & Nobles' Close the Book on Hate Initiative.
3. *Licensing,* as when a charity such as the World Wildlife Fund licenses the use of its name and logo to Visa. The company then donates a percentage of every transaction associated with the logo to the charity. Benefits of these relationships include allowing charities to raise much needed money and educate consumers, and helping corporations to increase their profits, bolster their reputations, and distinguish their brands. And it lets consumers feel that they are making a difference in the world (Eikenberry 2009, 52–53).

But are there hidden costs? Patricia M. Nickel and Angela M. Eikenberry (2009) use the term "consumption philanthropy" for these relationships. They suggest that the hidden costs include individualizing solutions to collective problems, replacing virtuous action with mindless buying, and hiding how markets create many social problems in the first place, thereby compromising the potential for charity to better society.

*Sources:* Eikenberry 2009; Nickel and Eikenberry 2009.

## References

Austin, J., H. Stevenson, and J. Wei-Skillern (2006). Social and commercial entrepreneurship: Same, different, or both? *Entrepreneurship Theory and Practice,* 30(1), 1–22.
Brinckerhoff, P.C. (1996). *Financial empowerment: More money for mission.* Dillon, CO: Alpine Guild.
———. (2000a). *Mission-based management: Leading your not-for-profit in the 21st century.* 2d ed. San Francisco: Jossey-Bass.
———. (2000b). *Social entrepreneurship: The art of mission-based venture development.* San Francisco: Jossey-Bass.
Caesar, P., and T. Baker (2004). Fundamental of implementation. In *Generating and sustaining nonprofit earned income: A guide to successful enterprise strategies,* ed. S.M. Oster, C.W. Massarsky, and S.L. Beinhacker, 207–223. San Francisco: Jossey-Bass.
Cordes, J.J., and C.E. Steuerle (2009). Nonprofits and business: A new world of innovation and adaptation. In *Nonprofits and Business,* ed. J.J. Cordes and C.E. Steuerle, 3–20. Washington, DC: Urban Institute.
Crisis Center of Tampa Bay (2010). TransCare ambulance services. www.crisiscenter.com/CoreServices/TransCareAmbulanceServices/tabid/77/Default.aspx.
Dees, J.G. (1998). Enterprising Nonprofits. *Harvard Business Review* (January–February), 55–67.
———. (2004). Putting nonprofit business ventures in perspective. In *Generating and sustaining nonprofit earned income: A guide to successful enterprise strategies,* ed. S.M. Oster, C.W. Massarsky, and S.L. Beinhacker, 3–18. San Francisco: Jossey-Bass.
Dees, J.G., J. Emerson, and P. Economy (2001). *Enterprising nonprofits: A toolkit for social entrepreneurs.* San Francisco: John Wiley & Sons.
———. (2002). *Strategic tools for social entrepreneurs: Enhancing the performance of your enterprising nonprofit.* San Francisco: John Wiley & Sons.
Dropkin, M., and A. Hayden (2001). *The cash flow management book for nonprofits: A step-by-step guide for managers, consultants, and boards.* San Francisco: Jossey-Bass.
Eikenberry, A.M. (2009). The hidden costs of cause marketing. *Stanford Social Innovation Review,* 7(3), 50–55.
Foster, W., and J. Bradach (2005). Should nonprofits seek profits? *Harvard Business Review.*

Gulf Coast Jewish Family Services Inc. & Gulf Coast Community Care Division (2008). Annual Report. Clearwater, Florida.

Higgins, G., and J. Finnie (2010). Scaling back or shutting down the venture. In *Succeeding at social enterprise: Hard-won lessons for nonprofits and social entrepreneurs,* ed. Social Enterprise Alliance, 227–241. San Francisco: Jossey-Bass.

Kirlin, J.A. (2006). Social enterprise in the United States and Europe: Understanding and learning form the differences. *Voluntas,* 17(3), 247–263.

Martin, L.L. (2001). *Financial management for human services.* Needham Heights, MA: Allyn & Bacon.

National Conference of State Legislatures (2009). The fiscal nightmare continues for states. December 9. www.ncsl.org/?tabid=19250.

Nickel, P.M., and A.M. Eikenberry (2009). A critique of the discourse of marketized philanthropy. *American Behavioral Scientist,* 52(7), 974–989.

Oster, S.M., C.W. Massarsky, and S.L. Beinhacker (eds.) (2004). *Generating and sustaining nonprofit earned income: A guide to successful enterprise strategies.* San Francisco: Jossey-Bass.

Pogrebin, R. (2009). In the arts, bigger buildings may not be better. *New York Times,* December 12, A1.

Schulte, E. (2009). New Goodwill store to pack style. *St. Petersburg Times,* May 18. www.tampabay.com/news/business/article1002097.ece.

Seedco (2007). *The limits of social enterprise: A field study and case analysis.* New York: Seedco Policy Center.

Strom, S. (2009). Civil liberties group loses $20 million donor. *New York Times,* December 9, 18A.

Surtel, M. (2009). Counties: Governor's aid delay not a surprise—and not welcome. *Daily News: Serving Genesee, Wyoming and Orleans Counties* (New York), December 15. /www.thedaileynewsonline.com/articles/2009/12/15/news/6282011.prt.

Timmons, E. (2009). State owes 2 local nonprofits $5M. *Galesburg Register-Mail,* December 24. www.galesburg.com/news/x664192652/State-owes-2-local-nonprofits-5M.

Wesibrod, B.A. (2004).The pitfalls of profits: Why nonprofits should get out of commercial ventures. *Stanford Social Innovation Review,* 2(3), 40–47.

Winder, V. (2009). Some states are delaying payments to nonprofits. April 30. Brief, Alliance for Children & Families and United Neighborhood Centers. http://alliance1.org/sites/default/files/pdf_upload/report_pp/prompt_payment.pdf.

Wing, K.T., K.L. Roeger, and T.H. Pollak (2010). *The nonprofit sector in brief: Public charities, giving, and volunteering, 2010.* Washington, DC: Urban Institute.

Wolk, A. (2008). Advancing social entrepreneurship: Recommendations for policy makers and government agencies. Washington, DC: Aspen Institute's Nonprofit Sector and Philanthropy Program.

Young, D.R. (2005). Mission-market tension in managing nonprofit organizations. Working paper 06–26, Andrew Young School of Policy Studies Research Paper Series. http://aysps.gsu.edu/publications/2006/downloads/Young_MissionMarketTension.pdf.

———. (2009). Alternative perspectives on social enterprise. In *Nonprofits and business,* ed. J.J. Cordes and C.E. Steuerle, 21–46. Washington, DC: Urban Institute.

# ——6——

# Organizational Effectiveness and Program Measurement
## Documenting Successes and Improving Performance

Nonprofit organizations are facing tough times. Scarce resources, budget deficits, and greater demands for services are challenging nonprofit administrators. Policy makers and funders are requiring that nonprofit programs demonstrate their effectiveness and impact on the individuals and communities that receive their services. With financial resources being reduced, decision makers no longer can continue to support all services and programs. Choices need to be made among competing services, programs, and agencies. Performance measurement systems, if developed and implemented correctly, can provide agency decision makers, policy makers, and funders with information to make informed decisions. Supporters of performance measurement believe that effective evaluations will indicate agency or program successes, enable agencies to share information with key constituencies, and assist in improving their services (Hatry 2006; Mattessich 2003; Poister 2003, United Way of America 1996).

Performance measurement systems provide agencies with information about how effective their programs are, what aspects of the programs are effective, and where the need for improvement lies. Through measurement and evaluation, agencies can measure the extent to which goals or objectives are met. Performance measurement refers to a variety of procedures used to track the performance of agency services and programs. Performance measures are objective indicators of various aspects of the performance of programs or agencies.

The language used to describe measuring the effectiveness or impact of programs can be confusing. Some researchers use the term *performance measurement systems* (Hatry 2006; Poister 2003), while others use the terms *program evaluation* and *outcome evaluation* to describe similar procedures (Mattessich 2003). Still others use the phrase *managing for results* (Newcomber 2007). Poister (2003) notes that performance measures are basic components of program evaluations and support the program evaluation function, along with other important management functions such as monitoring and reporting, strategic planning, budgeting and financial management, program management, quality improvement, process improvement, contract management, external benchmarking, and communication with stakeholders.

Nonprofits need to be familiar and comfortable with performance measurement. This chapter will provide a brief overview of organizational effectiveness and program measurement in the nonprofit sector, and it poses the following questions:

- How can measurement systems improve the effectiveness of non-profit programs and services?
- What role do funders play in developing measurement systems?
- What are the management challenges in implementing measurement systems?
- What are the management risks in not instituting measurement systems?

The growth of state and local governments' contracting with nonprofits to deliver services leads to increased accountability. Service agencies have been expected to be accountable for their expenditure of public contract funds (Rathgeb-Smith 2008), while the Government Performance and Results Act of 1993 (GPRA) requires federal agencies to measure and report on program performance. For example, the Healthy and Safe Families Act of 1997 requires the development of outcome measures to be used in allocating federal funds to state agencies involved in child welfare, a requirement that has been passed on to nonprofits. The GPRA defines program evaluation as "assessment, through objective measurement and systematic analyses, of the manner and extent to which federal programs achieve intended outcomes." Program evaluations include the needs assessment for programs, assessments of the compliance of program implementation with statutory guidance, and cost effectiveness of different program interventions (Newcomber 2007).

Regardless of the words used to describe the process, the purpose of performance measurement systems is to provide an evaluation of the impacts or results of agency programs (Fitzpatrick et al. 2004).

## Perceived Benefits of Measurement Systems

Some of the benefits identified in developing and implementing measurement systems include:

- Enabling agencies to learn from clients and constituents how they feel about the agency and its programs and how they think the programs help them.
- Illustrating the impacts and externalities of programs that were neither intended nor expected. These might include effects of services on constituents that go beyond what was intended. The impacts might include the effects of services on other individuals, families, or communities.
- Systematically gathering, compiling, and reviewing information over time. Agencies can then develop a more comprehensive understanding of how the populations served are changing; what issues, concerns, and needs they have; and how those needs might change over the years.
- Helping to communicate information with key stakeholders such as staff, volunteers, and funders about the positive impacts the programs have on individuals, their families, and the community.
- Enabling agencies to respond to requests for "outcome-based management" data.
- Helping agencies build on their successes and correct problems, which thus improves their services. Information acquired during the early stages of a program enable an agency to see how well it is reaching its targeted audiences and delivering intended services. With this information, programs can adjust to provide more of what works well and can search for alternatives for what does not.
- The identification of which programs or activities are most effective and should continue to receive funding or have their funding increased.

Agencies that can demonstrate what they are doing and how it makes a difference in the lives of individuals, families, and communities will be in a stronger position for funding (Hatry 2006; Hatry et al. 2006; Mattessich 2003; Poister 2003; United Way of America 1996; Urban Institute 2009, Wholey et al. 1994).

## Types of Evaluations

There are different types of evaluations; some of the most common found in the nonprofit sector are process, outcome, cost-benefit and cost-effectiveness, and developmental evaluations.

*Process evaluations* assess how the program operates and documents the procedures and activities undertaken in service delivery. Such evaluations help to identify problems faced in delivering services and strategies for overcoming these problems. They are useful for adapting or replicating program strategies. They analyze the extent to which a program is operating as it was intended. One question typically asked is "Are there ways the implementation of a program can be improved to better meet the program's objectives?" In addition, process evaluations often will assess program activities' conformance to statutory and regulatory requirements, program design, and professional standards or consumer expectations.

*Outcome evaluations* focus on the results of the program's activities. Did the program have the intended effects? Are objectives being met? Outcome evaluations are concerned with describing, exploring, or determining changes that occur in program recipients or secondary audiences such as the families of recipients, coworkers, or communities as a result of a program. The outcomes can range from an immediate impact or a final outcome or an unintended outcome. Outcome evaluation considers the long-term consequences of a program, assessing its actual effects on a problem.

*Cost-benefit* and *cost-effectiveness evaluations* compare a program's outputs or outcomes with the costs to produce them. Cost-benefit analysis aims to identify all relevant costs and benefits, usually expressed in dollar terms, to assess the total cost of meeting goals or outcomes.

*Developmental evaluations* include asking questions and gathering information to provide feedback and to support decision making and corrections as programs are being developed and implemented. The intent is for evaluations to be innovative instead of retrospective.

## Program Theory and Measurement

Program theory is a tool for understanding the program to be evaluated and guiding the evaluation. Chen defines program theory as "a specification of what must be done to achieve the desired goals, what other important impact may also be anticipated, and how these goals and impacts would be generated" (1990). Program theory consists of normative theory and causative theory. *Normative theory* describes the program as it *should be*, its goals and outcomes, its interventions and rationale from the perspectives of various stakeholders. *Causative theory* makes use of existing research to describe potential outcomes of the program based on characteristics of the clients and the program's actions. The information gained from these theories can then be used to develop a plausible program model. By expressing the theory of a program, the evaluator begins with an understanding of how the program is supposed to achieve its goals. In the early days of evaluation, it was not uncommon to find that program evaluations were developed only to comply with funding requirements and did not attempt to link assumptions or research with program activities (McGarvey 2007; Fitzpatrick et al. 2004, 205). Mattessich (2003, 27) notes that program theory enables managers to link evaluation information in a meaningful way; to understand why something works, not just to see whether it works; to apply knowledge to new situations; to understand what additional information is needed and what can be omitted to improve programs over time and meet the mission of the organization.

## Developing a Program Description

Performance measurement typically begins by describing the program or services under review. Fitzpatrick et al. note the following:

> A program description is a description of the critical elements of the program to be evaluated. Such a description typically includes goals and objectives, critical components and activities, and descriptions of the target audience. It may also include characteristics of personnel delivering the program, administrative arrangements, the physical setting, and other contextual factors. The critical factor in a program description is that it is sufficiently detailed to provide the evaluator with an understanding of why the program is supposed to achieve its desired impacts and to serve as a foundation for identifying evaluation questions. An accurate description agreed upon by all stakeholders provides a common understanding of the program for all the parties involved, permitting the evaluation to proceed with some consensus concerning the entity to be examined.

Some of the factors warranting consideration include identifying:
- What is the program all about?
- What are its objectives, evaluation criteria, and clientele groups?

- What are its major components and activities, its basic structure, and administrative and managerial design?
- What research exists to link the activities of the program and characteristics of the clients with the desired outcomes?
- What is the program's setting and context (geographical, demographic, political, level of generality)?
- Who participates in the program (direct and indirect participants, program deliverers, managers and administrators, policy makers)?
- What critical decisions are key stakeholders facing in regard to the program? What is the time line for these decisions?
- Are there contextual events such as contract negotiations, budgetary decisions, or changes in administration that could affect the program in ways that might distort the evaluation? (Fitzpatrick et al. 2004, 203–204; Hatry 2006; Mattessich 2003)

## Logic Models

The United Way of America, the Urban Institute, the Center of What Works, along with a variety of other nonprofits and foundations, have developed logic models to evaluate programs. A logic model starts with the long-term vision of how program participants, secondary individuals (i.e., family members, teachers), or the community will be better off (changed) because of the program. It asks, "Are participants or target groups better off after service than they were before?" (United Way of America 1996, 18).

The Center for What Works (2009) and the Urban Institute (2009) have compiled lists of the best outcome indictors and developed standardized logic models for fourteen program areas: Adult Education and Family Literacy; Advocacy; Affordable Housing; Assisted Living; Business Assistance; Community Organizing; Emergency Shelters; Employment Training; Health Risk Reduction; Performing Arts; Prison Reentry; Transitional Housing; Youth Mentoring; and Youth Tutoring.

$$\text{Inputs} \rightarrow \text{Activities} \rightarrow \text{Outputs} \rightarrow \text{Outcomes}$$

*Inputs* are the resources dedicated to or consumed by the activity; for example, money, staff and staff time, facilities, equipment and supplies, volunteers, and volunteer time. They can also be constraints on the program or service, such as laws, regulations, and funder's requirements.

*Activities* are what the staff or program does to fulfill its mission; for example, provide fire safety training, create mentoring relationships for youth, or provide swimming lessons.

*Outputs* are the direct products or services provided by activities, such as the number of resident meetings, presentations made to civic groups, the number of children enrolled in child care, the number of individuals enrolled in anger-management classes. Outputs do not constitute direct benefits but are essential because they lead to outcomes. They are the immediate products or services produced. However, there is no guarantee that the desired outcomes will be attained through the production of outputs.

*Outcomes* are the results that you hope will an agency's program action. They are the benefits that occur during and after the activity or intervention. For example, fewer public health risks, less criminal activity by youth, new knowledge, increased skills, changed attitudes or values, modified behavior, some improved condition or altered status.

## Performance Measures

A variety of measures are used to evaluate service or program effectiveness. The most common measures in nonprofit organizations are the following:

*Resource measures* are resources supporting a program that can be measured in their own units (number of counselors, nurses, trainers, ball fields, computer work stations). Resources are not produced by a program or service, they are investments in the front end, but when your focus is on improving the mix or quality of resources, it may be appropriate to track resources as indicators of performance. Typically resources are used for computing efficiency measures such as the cost per hour of recreational instruction, or cost-effectiveness measures such as the cost per participant who develops a skill.

*Workload measures* represent the flow of cases into a system or numbers of participants who need to be served; for example, the number of days required to process applications for health services.

*Output measures* determine the volume of program or service activities such as the hours of counseling sessions conducted by a social service agency. They are sometimes measured in terms of the amount of work that is performed, such as the number of story hours that preschool staff conduct. Sometimes, they may be the number of cases dealt with by a program, such the number of clients or families carried by social workers.

*Productivity measures* most often measure the rate of production per a specific unit of resource, usually staff. To be meaningful they are defined in some unit of time, such as the number of calls each crisis hotline employee receives per hour. Sometimes the specific resources used may measure equipment rather than personnel, such as the number of computers used in the Boys & Girls Club per day, the number of hours or days a community room is used by the public, and the number of days that camp pavilions are rented out.

*Efficiency measures* relate outputs to the resources utilized in producing them, but efficiency ratios look at the ratio of outputs to the dollar costs of the collective resources consumed in producing them—for example, the cost per each crisis hotline call.

*Service quality measures* pertain most directly to service delivery processes and outputs, because they define the service that is being provided. It is important not just to think of how much output is provided (quantity), but also to examine the quality of the outputs. Sometimes measures of service quality are based on standard operating procedures that are prescribed for service delivery processes.

*Effectiveness measures* represent the degree to which a program or agency is producing its intended outcome and achieving the desired results. The most important effectiveness measures relate back to the basic purpose of a given program.

*Cost-effectiveness measures* relate costs to outcome measures. These are different from efficiency measures, which are unit costs of producing outputs. Cost-effectiveness of smoking cessation programs would be the costs associated with a person improving her health.

*Consumer satisfaction measures* focus on program outputs—asking the participants of a recreation program if they were satisfied with the programs they participated in; asking symphony patrons if they were satisfied with the number and selection of performances offered by the orchestra.

## Why the Resistance to Performance Measurement?

Despite the noted benefits of performance measurement, one only has to read publications such as the *Chronicle of Philanthropy,* the *Nonprofit Quarterly*, and *Stanford Social Innovation Review* to view opposing opinions or articles on the merits of research and evaluation. Some of the most commonly cited reasons for opposing performance measurement are given below.

Many nonprofit agencies provide services to vulnerable individuals, who may be poor, illiterate, homeless, the victims of domestic violence, suffering from mental illness or other health problems, or unemployed. These problems are difficult to solve, and it may take years to determine the programs' and services' success, which can make it difficult to evaluate many of them.

Many programs in health and human services focus on prevention of unhealthy activity such as drug or alcohol abuse and violence behavior, but successful prevention cannot be measured.

Nonprofits in such fields as social welfare, health, and education operate in complicated environments and often must contend with inconsistent public policies, political environments, competing constituencies, and funding over which they have little control.

There is also the concern that evaluations will invite unfair comparisons to other agencies' programs, that performance data will be used against the program, that agencies don't have the data or cannot obtain it, and/or that the agency's staff is already stretched too thin to collect the data.

Many administrators believe that the value of their programs cannot be measured, or that conducting program evaluations is too time consuming and expensive to undertake. In regard to foundations, one researcher found that staff members saw internal evaluations taking time away from other important activities such as meeting with prospective grant seekers, analyzing proposals, and keeping up with developments in their respective fields, and that they instinctively distrusted external evaluators, who were perceived as undermining their professional autonomy (David 2006).

In another study, researchers found mixed results in regard to the importance of performance measurement. A small sample of individual donors who earned their wealth in finance and investing are not particularly interested in receiving better data on the performance of nonprofit organizations. Instead, they tend to rely on personal connections in deciding to make donations—the imperative to give is based on a trusting relationship with a nonprofit executive or board member and not on performance data. However, institutional funders do rely on performance measurement data; they want their donors and trustees to feel confident that money is being spent wisely. Also, some nonprofit executives find that by having performance data, they can combine the objective data with anecdotes about the impact and success of the organizations (Cunningham and Ricks 2004).

A common complaint about performance measurement is that often the required data does not accurately capture performance. Nonprofits receiving money from a number of funders have to track and compile different data, requests for information, and complete reports that differ substantially across funders. If better coordination among funders, and between funders and nonprofits, existed, it could alleviate some of the time-consuming and labor-intensive demands on direct service organizations (David 2006; Meissner 1999).

A number of difficult issues are raised when measuring and evaluating programs. What kind of evaluations should be conducted? Should developmental evaluations be used to help organizations improve, or should outcome evaluations be used to determine whether there was an impact on participants or communities? Should the measurements be qualitative or quantitative? Should evaluators come from within the organization or outside? Should the agency be evaluated or individual programs? Often, even larger foundations disagree on the meaning of key evaluation terms. Funders have their own definitions, methods, and measures. Many nonprofits spend time tailoring their reporting to each funder's requirements (Snibbe 2006, 40).

Strictly controlled experimental designs are hard to implement. Research designs need a control group, and random assignments are expensive. Some of the participants do not receive the treatment, and nonprofit administrators are reluctant to withhold services. They believe if a health or social service program is in the best interest of a participant, they should receive the service (Snibbe 2006).

Success indicators may be different across types of nonprofits. Scholars such as Sowa et al. (2004) make distinctions between processes, structures and outputs, and between management capacity and program capacity. While Herman and Renz (1997) note that assessing performance is complicated because it is multidimensional and socially constructed, different stakeholders have different views and competing values. Ebrahim (2010) notes that nonprofit leadership needs to prioritize among competing accountability demands. This involves deciding to whom and for what they owe accountability (2). Upwards accountability refers to relationships with donors, foundations, and governments and is often focused on the use of funds. Downward accountability refers to relationships with clients and groups receiving services and may refer to communities indirectly impacted by nonprofit programs. Internal accountability refers to nonprofits themselves and centers on an organization's responsibility to its mission and staff, which includes decision makers as well as field-level implementers (4). To whom one is accountable varies, and measuring social value is difficult even when social return on investments (SROI) metrics are used (Mulgan 2010).

### *Those in Favor of Performance Measurement*

McCambridge (2006) believes "the best organizations have a natural hunger to know about how they are doing; how others are doing things, and with what results" (11–12). She identifies the types of research that should be undertaken in any effective organization:

- Informal but continuous and documented inquiry by everyone about community/constituent issues;
- Systematic surveying and research on community outreach/constituent issues, opinions, needs, and desires;
- Research about emerging trends in and influences on your environments;
- Research about the research in your field, programmatic models being tried elsewhere in similar fields, ideas floated, policy being proposed, outcomes achieved, and the variables believed to have affected those outcomes;
- Research about financial models used in similar organizations;
- Research about resources;
- Evaluation of individual programs and outcomes in measurement;
- Evaluation of organizational fit to the environment and organizational performance against mission;
- Research on management and governance ideas that may help organizations to function better.

The executive director of Big Brothers of Massachusetts Bay (BBMB), John Pearson, has persuaded individual donors to give more because the organization was able to link performance metrics with the impact on children's lives. By possessing data on its program's impacts, BBMB is able to provide specific answers to questions. He believes the measurement system has helped his organization become more scientific and accurate in its decisions.

> In human and social service organizations, too often feeling good about a particular approach has driven decision making. When there is a good performance management system that is properly designed, decision

making can focus more on "doing good." Data has changed the focus of discussion and has provided solid support for the sometimes hard but necessary decisions . . . it is clear that there are different factors that donors use in making their decision on where and how much to give. In my experience at BBMB, particularly on larger donations, good data and a good performance management culture are in the top three reasons donors continue and increase their contribution to a major gift. (Cited in Cunningham and Ricks 2004, 48)

While not discussing performance measurement or evaluation per se, Pfeffer and Sutton believe that evidence-based management can help managers figure out what works and what does not, identify dangerous half-truths that constitute so much of what passes for wisdom, and reject the total nonsense that too often passes for sound advice (2006, 40). Often individuals have preconceived ideas that make them oblivious to the facts. They need to understand that assumptions may be incorrect and may need to be rethought.

## Ethics and Performance Measurement

Hatry et al. (1994) emphasize that certain norms should guide all evaluators' work. Evaluators should ensure that criteria are relevant and that findings will be available in time for important policy and management decisions. Within the available resource constraints, it is important to ensure that data conclusions are valid. Evaluators should ensure adequate training for data collectors, pretests of data collection schemes, ongoing quality-control testing of data collection, and security of the resulting data.

Regardless of who sponsors the evaluation, evaluators should seek input from program managers and staff on objectives and criteria. Where appropriate, evaluators should include the program manager and key program staff on the evaluation team, or as reviewers of the evaluation design and draft reports. Program managers should be kept aware of the progress of evaluations and be given the opportunity to review evaluation findings before they are made public (Hatry et al. 1994, 594).

## Conclusion

Performance measurement is the systematic examination of specific services or programs to provide information on their impact. It concentrates on outcomes, identifying how community, social, or individual conditions have changed as a result of specific services or sets of activities. It attempts to measure the degree to which a program is achieving its intended purposes. It helps decide whether a program should be continued, expanded, modified, reduced, or eliminated. If a program is not performing as desired, the performance measurement or program evaluations may help indicate the reasons for ineffectiveness and the actions that might be taken to remedy the situation. While performance measurements may be threatening to the administrators whose programs are being evaluated, a major purpose of evaluation is to provide information that will help agency managers and staff to improve their programs. However, there are challenges in performance measurement or program evaluation that need to be recognized. Effective communication among stakeholders is important. There should be agreement as to the agency's or program's objectives and what would be relevant performance measures. Mulgan (2010, 43) notes that measures of social value should distinguish between those required for external accountability, those that help internal management, and those that support assessments of the broader patterns of social impact. Confronting questions related to strategy, capital, and talent is important (Bradach et al. 2008). Identifying specific objectives can result in political challenges because key stakeholders may have different values and priorities. These challenges should not deter agency leaders from performance measurement. Evaluating the effectiveness of programs is good management. Agency leaders need feedback to guide future decisions regarding agency services and programs.

---

### Case 6.1. Could a Performance Measurement System Help New York City's Foster Care System?

More than twenty years ago, New York City attempted to create and support a foster care system that would protect its black and Latino children. It was thought that agencies run by persons of color and embedded in the neighborhoods and communities where the children came from would be more sensitive to the children's needs. More recently, New York City's child welfare commissioner aimed to bring accountability to the dozens of private agencies the city paid hundreds of millions of dollars each year to care for foster children. Evidence of fraud, mismanagement, and mistreatment of children led him to end contracts with two of the city's largest neighborhood-based, minority-run foster care agencies. Six minority agencies were placed on notice that they would be investigated and possibly closed. They were ranked at the bottom of the approximately forty agencies funded by the city. One agency, Family Support Systems Unlimited Inc., identified by the city as troubled, suggested that the city's system for evaluating its foster care agencies was flawed and that the city was unwilling to acknowledge that agencies like itself were often left to deal with the most challenging and unwanted children. Churches, local politicians, and families rallied to save Family Support Systems Unlimited Inc. The poor evaluation scores reflected problems across more than one dozen measures, from levels of abuse in foster homes to adoption rates to how well the agencies kept track of whether children were fed and clothed, attending school, and receiving medical attention.

The child welfare commissioner set up a task force to study the experiences of the city's minority agencies and promised to study their recommendations as to how the agencies would be preserved and supported. Some on the task force panel felt the commissioner's decision to place six out of eight minority agencies under review was brazen and insensitive, and felt that the move had imperiled a modest network at a time when almost all of the city's 18,000 foster children were black or Latino.

The task force members, who came from diverse racial and professional backgrounds, were largely in agreement on the unique attributes of minority agencies, their cultural sensitivity, and their locations in needy neighborhoods as well as their struggle for money and survival. All of the agencies were founded on "a wing and a prayer." One task force member said there had been a "persistent lack of understanding" of the "culture, needs, and strengths of children and families of color." Another member was not convinced of the need to keep every minority agency: "My view was, you look at the performance of the agency, and you keep the agencies that are performing well." He also agreed that minority agencies were critical to the system even if they were not the peak performers, and he acknowledged that the city's evaluation system had its own problems. For example, the system awarded points to agencies for the number of adoptions they completed and how fast they were done. Yet minority agencies argue that black and Latino children sometimes benefited from staying in stable long-term foster care with a relative rather than being placed for adoption with a stranger. That philosophy could cost the agency points. Another task force member, a former executive director of the Federation of Protestant Welfare Agencies, noted that "in this field, as in many other fields, numbers do not always tell the story."

*Source:* Kaufman 2007; Kaufman and Weiser 2007; Weiser 2007.

---

## Case 6.2. Measuring Hope's Success Tricky

Pinellas Hope operates a tent city for homeless people in Florida. The leaders of Hope City list the benefits of the program as providing food, shelter, and the opportunity to receive services. The tent city was created by the county, city, and private groups to ease rising homelessness and the complaints from city residents. A survey of the pilot phase was conducted for 371 people who were discharged from the program six months after staying at the tent city between December 2007 and April 2008. Many of the others residents could not be tracked down, did not respond to the survey, or left the local area. Thirteen percent returned to Pinellas Hope, wanted no contact, or went to jail; 16 percent maintained housing; 22 percent had a wrong phone number; and 49 percent left without housing. Pinellas Hope organizers acknowledge that they need to do a better job of tracking the population they serve. They have begun discussions with the county to see if the county's 211-community voice mail system can be used to connect with the former residents after they leave.

*Source:* DeCamp 2009.

## Case 6.3. Why Don't Nonprofits Evaluate the Results of Their Marketing Efforts?

A study of the use of marketing by nonprofits found that the biggest goal of the effort is to make the public aware of their organizations and the second is to raise money. Charities thought the best way to build awareness of their organizations was through articles and broadcasts about them in the news media and efforts to get the attention of government officials and other leaders who could influence public opinion.

They confessed, however, that they did not know how effective their marketing is. Twenty-five percent of the respondents admitted that they do not try to measure the effectiveness of many types of marketing techniques.

*Source:* Schwinn 2008.

# References

Bradach, J.L., T.J. Tierney, and N. Stone (2008). Delivering on the promise of nonprofits. *Harvard Business Review*, 86(12), 88–97.

Center for What Works (2009). WhatWorks toolkits. www.whatworks.org/display-common.cfm?an=1&subarticlenbr=13.

Chen, H. (1990). Issues in constructing program theory. *New Directions for Program Evaluation*, 47, 7–12.

Cunningham, K., and M. Ricks (2004). Why should nonprofits measure? *Stanford Social Innovation Review*, 2(1), 44–51.

David, T. (2006). Evaluation and foundations: Can we have an honest conversation? *Nonprofit Quarterly*, 13(10), 90–93.

DeCamp, D. (2009). Measuring Pinellas Hope project's success is proving difficult. *St. Petersburg Times*, May 10. www.tampabay.com/news/localgovernment/article999390.ece.

Ebrahim, A. (2010). The many faces of nonprofit accountability. Working paper 10–069. Cambridge, MA: Harvard Business School.

Fitzpatrick, J.L., J.R. Sanders, and B.R. Worthen (2004). *Program evaluation: Alternative approaches and practical guidelines*. 3rd ed. Boston: Pearson.

Hatry, H.P. (2006). *Performance measurement: Getting results*. 2nd ed. Washington, DC: Urban Institute Press.

Hatry, H.P., D.M. Fisk, J.R. Hall Jr., P.S. Schaenman, and L. Snyder (2006). *How effective are your community services? Procedures for performance measurement*. 3rd ed. Washington, DC: ICMA and the Urban Institute.

Hatry, H.P., K.G. Newcomber, and J.S. Wholey (1994). Conclusion: Improving evaluation activities and results. In *The handbook of practical program evaluation*, ed. J.S. Wholey, H.P. Hatry, and K.E. Newcomber, 590–601. San Francisco: Jossey-Bass.

Herman, R., and D. Renz (1997). Multiple constituencies and the social construction of organizational effectiveness. *Nonprofit and Voluntary Sector Quarterly*, 26(2), 185–206.

Kaufman, L. (2007). A history of neglect: Foster children at risk, and opportunity lost. *New York Times*, November 5, A1. www.nytimes.com/2007/11/05/nyregion/05foster.html.

Kaufman, L., and B. Weiser (2007). A history of neglect: In foster care review, vows of help and vigilance. *New York Times*, November 7, A1. www.nytimes.com/2007/11/07/nyregion/07foster.html.

Mattessich, P.W. (2003). *The manager's guide to program evaluation: Planning, contracting, and managing for useful results*. St. Paul, MN: Wilder.

McCambridge, R. (2006). Research and nonprofit excellence. *Nonprofit Quarterly*, 13(1), 11–17.

McGarvey, C. (2007). Mapping change: Using a theory of change to guide planning and evaluation. Grantcraft. http://impact.animatingdemocracy.org/node/452.

Meissner, R. (1999). Charity evaluation: More of a luxury than many people care to admit. *Chronicle of Philanthropy*, March 11, 46.

Mulgan, G. (2010). Measuring social value. *Stanford Social Innovation Review*, 8(3), 38–43.

Newcomber, K.E. (2007). Measuring government performance. *International Journal of Public Administration,* 30, 307–29.

Pfeffer, J., and R.I. Sutton (2006). Act on facts, not faith. *Stanford Social Innovation Review,* 4(1), 38–45.

Poister, T.H. (2003). *Measuring performance in public and nonprofit organizations.* San Francisco: Jossey-Bass.

Rathgeb-Smith, S. (2008). The challenge of strengthening nonprofits and civil society. *Public Administration Review,* S68, S132–S145.

Schwinn, E. (2008). Most charities don't evaluate results of marketing efforts, new study finds. *Chronicle of Philanthropy,* 20(9) (July 24), 23.

Snibbe, A.C. (2006). Drowning in data: Most nonprofit evaluation hurts more than it helps. *Stanford Social Innovation Review,* 4(3), 38–45.

Sowa, J., S. Selden, and J. Sandifort (2004). No longer unmeasureable? A multidimensional integrated model of nonprofit organizational effectiveness. *Nonprofit and Voluntary Sector Quarterly,* 33(4), 711–28.

United Way of America (1996). *Measuring program outcomes: A practical approach.* Alexandria, VA: Author.

Urban Institute (2009). Outcome indicators project. www.urban.org/center/cnp/projects/outcomeindicators.cfm.

Weiser, B. (2007). A history of neglect; City slow to act as hope for foster children fails. *New York Times,* November 6, A1. www.nytimes.com/2007/11/06/nyregion/06foster2.html.

Wholey, J.S., H.P. Hatry, and K.E. Newcomber (eds.) (1994). *Handbook of practical program evaluation.* San Francisco: Jossey-Bass.

# ———7———

# Human Resources Management
## What Makes Nonprofits Different?

Human resource management (HRM) is the design of formal systems in an organization to ensure the effective use of employees' knowledge, skills, abilities, and other characteristics (KSAOCs) to accomplish organizational goals. It concerns the recruitment, selection, training and development, compensation and benefits, retention, evaluation, and promotion of employees, and labor-management relations within an organization.

The technical aspects of nonprofit human resources management are similar to the techniques used in the public and for-profit sectors. For example, the laws and techniques governing job analysis, performance evaluations, compensation and benefits, training and development, labor-management relations, and human resources information systems are typically similar. What is different is the context in which they take place. For a comprehensive review of strategic nonprofit human resources management, see *Human Resources Management for Public and Nonprofit Organizations* (Pynes 2009).

Consider the following:

> The city commission of Tarpon Springs, Florida, voted unanimously to allow hiring decisions to be based on religious beliefs at Helen Ellis Hospital. It voted to approve a request by Adventist Health Systems Sunbelt, which is associated with the Seventh-day Adventist Church, to waive a clause in their lease agreement with the hospital that prohibited discrimination on religion. The vote will enable Adventist Health System to finalize its merger with University Community Hospital Inc., which operates the hospital. Other changes would make it so nonemergency workers will not have to work and no major medical procedures will be conducted from sundown Friday to sundown Saturday in keeping with the Seventh-day Adventist religious beliefs. Adventist is the largest nonprofit Protestant health care system in the nation, sponsored by the Seventh-day Adventist Church. The system has 38 hospitals in 12 states. (Lee 2010)

A board member of a Catholic nonprofit was told that he could not become board president because he is gay. Jeffrey Goldone, who has been a vice president of the Society of St. Vincent de Paul of St. Louis board of directors for five years, was nominated for president. He accepted the nomination but could not be considered and was told that his living relationship goes against Catholic moral teaching. The group's executive director, Zip Rzeppa, wrote in an e-mail, "We serve all people without discrimination. And please note we are not discriminating against Jeff Goldone, a man who has done much good. He disqualified himself for the position of president by choosing to live a lifestyle of illicit sexual union, which falls outside the teachings of the Catholic Church, and outside the qualifications of the Society's International Rule" (cited in Bogan 2010).

St. Louis archbishop Robert Carlson in a statement to the *St. Louis Post Dispatch* said, "The Society of St. Vincent de Paul has a regulation that members running for president live a life according to church teaching. I clarified what church teaching is in the matter of homosexuality" (cited in Bogan 2010).

Fifty-one percent of top fund-raising executive positions are held by women at the nation's top charities, while 6.9 percent are minorities (Joslyn 2010). Only 7.6 percent of chief executives or chief giving officers at foundations are minorities, and only 14 percent of the board members of foundations are minorities (Morning and Tansimore 2010).

This chapter will answer the following questions:

- How is human resources management in the nonprofit sector different than in public or for-profit agencies?
- Why is it lawful for religiously affiliated nonprofits to discriminate on the basis of religion?
- What are the expressive rights of voluntary organizations?
- How important are volunteers to nonprofit organizations?
- What are some of the leadership and diversity challenges facing nonprofit organizations?

## Religious Discrimination and Nonprofits

### Title VII of the Civil Rights Act of 1964

Title VII of the Civil Rights Act of 1964 forbids any employer to fail to hire, to discharge, or to classify employees, or to discriminate with respect to compensation, terms, conditions, or privileges of employment in any way that would deprive any individual of employment opportunity due to race, color, religion, sex, or national origin. However, there are exemptions to Title VII that specifically state employers may discriminate on the basis of sex, religion, or national origin if the characteristic can be justified as a "bona fide occupational qualification [BFOQ] reasonably necessary to the normal operation of the particular enterprise" (Title VII, Sec. 703e).

Nonprofit organizations that provide secular services but are affiliated with and governed by religious institutions are exempt from the law under Section 702 of the Civil Rights Act of 1964, which states: "This title shall not apply to an employer with respect to the employment of aliens outside any State, or to *a religious corporation, association, educational institution, or society with respect to the employment of individuals of a particular religion to perform work connected with the carrying on by such corporation, association, educational institution, or society of its activities* (as amended by P.L. 92–261, eff. March 24, 1972).

Section 703(e)(1), (2) provides exemptions for educational institutions to hire employees of a particular religion if the institution is owned, controlled, or managed by a particular religious society. The exemption is broad and is not restricted to the religious activities of the institution.

In *Corporation of Presiding Bishop v. Amos* (1987), the Supreme Court upheld the right of the Mormon Church to terminate a building engineer who had worked at its nonprofit gymnasium for sixteen years, because he failed to maintain his qualification for church membership. The Court claimed that the decision to terminate was based on religion by the religious organization and thus exempted from the Title VII prohibition against religious discrimination.

Although the language of Title VII allows religious or faith-based organizations to discriminate on religious grounds only, courts have interpreted the religious exemptions to Title VII more broadly. The courts have also read a "ministerial exception" into Title VII under the Free Exercise Clause, which allows religious organizations to discriminate on gender, race, age, and conduct that is inconsistent with the tenets and teachings of the religious institution (Gossett and Pynes 2003; Pynes 2009, 2012).

*Pedreira v. Kentucky Baptist Homes for Children* (2001) was a federal district court case that addressed the personnel policies of a religiously affiliated nonprofit organization that provides government-funded social services. The U.S. district judge ruled that Kentucky Baptist Homes for Children (KBHC) was not guilty of religious discrimination when it fired Alicia Pedreira. The judge found that any discrimination practiced against Pedreira was due to her sexual orientation, not her religion, and rejected the argument that because her dismissal was motivated by KBHC's religious tenets, it constituted discrimination on the basis of religion. KBHC did not, the judge noted, establish any religious tests for its employees, nor are they required to attend religious services or be members or believers in any particular religion or religious group. The decision stated that Title VII "does not forbid an employer from having a religious motivation for discharging somebody because of some other trait or conduct not covered under the law. While KBHC seeks to employ only persons who adhere to a behavioral code consistent with KBHC's religious mission, the absence of religious requirements leaves their focus on behavior, not religion. KBHC imposes upon its employees a code of conduct which requires consistency with KBHC's religious beliefs, but not the beliefs themselves; the civil rights statute protects religious freedoms, not personal lifestyle choices" (*Pedreira v. Kentucky Baptist Homes for Children* 2001, 4–5). Because KBHC did not select employees based on religion nor required them to hold particular religious beliefs, the judge instead concluded that KBHC engaged in discrimination based on behavior and lifestyle choices (sexual orientation), which is not protected by Kentucky or federal law (Gossett and Pynes 2003; Pynes 2009, 2012).

In some cases, the courts have expanded the definition of clergy to include lay employees of religious institutions whose primary duties consist of teaching, spreading the faith, governance, supervision of religious order, or supervision or participation in religious ritual and worship. This means civil courts have ruled that the First Amendment prevents the civil courts from applying civil rights law to the relationship between a church and a minister. There have been mixed holdings in recent court cases in regard to the ministerial exception. Some have upheld it, while others have not (*Coulee Catholic Schools v. Labor and Industry Review Commission* 2009; *Petruska v. Gannon University* 2006a, 2006b; *Tomic v. Catholic Diocese of Peoria* 2006).

### Public Funding of Religiously Affiliated Nonprofits: Charitable Choice and Faith-Based Initiatives

"Charitable choice" was included as part the Personal Responsibility and Work Opportunity Reconciliation Act of 1996 (PRWORA). States could enter into funding relationships with any faith-based institution to provide social services using federal TANF (Temporary Assistance for Needy Families) dollars. "Charitable choice" permits religious organizations or faith-based organizations to receive federal funds for use in providing social services to their communities. As recipients of federal funds, they still retain their autonomy as independent organizations, while remaining in control of their religious mission and their organizational structure and governance. Faith-based organizations have a right to display religious art, scripture, and icons and retain their right to use religious criteria in hiring, firing, and disciplining employees. However, none of the funds received to provide services may be "expended for sectarian worship, instruction, or proselytization." Charitable choice explicitly prohibits participating faith-based organizations from denying services to people on the basis of religion, a religious belief, or refusal to actively participate in a religious practice. Clients who feel they are discriminated against can bring civil suits against providers (De Vita 1999).

To further expand the use of religious organizations and religion-affiliated nonprofits in the delivery of public services, President George W. Bush signed executive orders requiring executive branch agencies to identify and remove barriers that served as a deterrent to faith-based organizations in participating in executive agency programs. These executive orders are referred to as "faith-based initiatives." The executive orders established the White House Office of Faith-Based and Community Initiatives, as well as offices in more than ten government agencies.

In the case of *Lown v. the Salvation Army* (2005), filed in the U.S. District Court, Southern District of New York, the court ruled that the Salvation Army did not unlawfully discriminate on the basis of religion with respect to its professional employees working in child welfare services funded by New York State and New York City. The plaintiffs charged that the Army's New York division forced them to sign forms revealing the churches they had attended over the past ten years, name their ministers, and agree to the Army's mission "to preach the Gospel of Jesus Christ." (*Lown v. the Salvation Army, Inc.; Commission, New York City Administration for Children Services and others,* 2005). The court held that religious entities are exempted by Section 702 of the Civil Rights Act of 1964, and by comparable exemptions in the law of most states. The court concluded that the exemption represented a reasonable accommodation, within the discretion of Congress, of the interests of religious entities in their employment-centered exercise of religion and that the reasoning in *Corporation of Presiding Bishop v. Amos* (1987) extends fully to comparable state law provisions protecting the right of faith-based organizations to engage in faith-selective hiring for some or all positions (Lupu and Tuttle 2005; Pynes 2012).

The Civil Rights Act of 1964 and the executive orders allow federally funded religious or faith-based organizations to consider religion in the selection of employees whether the jobs to be performed are sectarian or not, even when the religion-affiliated or faith-based nonprofits are operating under contracts from the government. While faith-based service providers are permitted to require applicants to be a member of a particular denomination in hiring personnel, they are still prohibited from discriminating on the basis of race, gender, disability, or national origin.

On February 5, 2009, President Obama signed *Amendments to Executive Order 13199 and Establishment of the President's Advisory Council for Faith-Based and Neighborhood Partnerships* to help address the country's social problems by strengthening the capacity of faith-based and community organizations. The executive order does not reverse President Bush's policy that allowed federal agencies to award contracts to faith-based organizations that discriminate in their hiring processes based on religious status, marital status, or sexual orientation. In fact, President Obama has been criticized by the American Civil Liberties Union (ACLU) and the Coalition Against Religious Discrimination from backing down from his pledge during his campaign to reverse faith-based employment discrimination in publicly funded programs (American Civil Liberties Union 2010); however, conservatives are pleased with the direction the White House is taking (Wallsten 2010).

Most recently, a coalition of more than 100 religion-based nonprofits sent a letter to Congress to protest a provision in legislation presently being considered that would prohibit religion-affiliated nonprofits that receive federal funding from considering a job applicant's religion when making hiring decisions.

The pending legislation is the reauthorization of the Substance Abuse and Mental Health Services Administration (SAMSA) grant, which makes grants to social service nonprofits. World Vision, the Union of Orthodox Jewish Congregations of America, the U.S. Conference of Catholic Bishops, and the Southern Baptist Convention are some of the organizations opposed to eliminating the right to discriminate. Some of the nonprofits that do not believe the pending legislation goes far enough in preventing religious discrimination include Americans United for the Separation of Church and State, the Coalition Against Religious Discrimination, the Hindu American Foundation, the American Civil Liberties Union, and the NAACP (Flandez 2010; Posner 2010; Strom 2010).

## The Expressive Rights of Voluntary Organizations

Nonprofits are often referred to as voluntary organizations because they receive much of their financial support from private contributions and depend on volunteers to contribute their time and energies for public benefit. Because of their voluntary nature, which is reinforced by the First Amendment's protection of the freedom of association, nonprofits are often considered exempt from the application of nondiscrimination laws.

An organization's "expressive rights of association" refer to the right to associate for the purpose of engaging in those activities protected by the First Amendment: the right to speech, assembly, petition for the redress of grievances, and the exercise of religion. Any government intervention to regulate an organization's internal operations, such as membership or personnel policies, must be balanced against the organization's expressive rights of association. Nondiscrimination laws that force organizations to accept members whom they may not desire have been held by some courts to violate an organization's freedom of expressive association if the organization can demonstrate that these new members would affect in a significant way the group's ability to carry out its mission and express its private viewpoints (*Board of Directors, Rotary International v. Rotary Club of Duarte* 1987; *Boy Scouts of America and Monmouth Council v. James Dale* 2000; *Hurley v. Irish-American Gay Group of Boston* 1995; *New York State Club Association v. City of New York* 1988).

The U.S. Supreme Court in a 5–4 decision held that the application of New Jersey's public accommodation law to the Boy Scouts violated the Scouts' First Amendment expressive right of association (*Boy Scouts of America and Monmouth Council v. James Dale* 2000). The Boy Scouts argued successfully that, as a private organization, it has the right to determine criteria for membership. The Supreme Court heard this case on appeal from the Boy Scouts of America in response to the New Jersey Supreme Court's decision against its position.

The New Jersey Supreme Court held that the Boy Scouts of America is a place of "public accommodation" that "emphasizes open membership" and therefore must follow New Jersey's antidiscrimination law. The court further held that the state's law did not infringe upon the group's freedom of expressive association (*Dale v. Boy Scouts of America and Monmouth Council Boy Scouts* 1998, 1999). The court reasoned that the New Jersey legislature, when it enacted the antidiscrimination law, declared that discrimination is a matter of concern to the government and that infringements on that right may be justified by regulations adopted to serve compelling state interests (Hostetler and Pynes 2000a, 2000b).

On June 23, 2010, a federal jury decided that the City of Philadelphia violated the Boy Scouts' First Amendment right by using the Scouts' anti-gay policy as a reason to evict them from the city-owned offices (Gorenstein 2010). The city had requested the Cradle of Liberty Council to publicly renounce its membership policy against people who are openly homosexual or atheists if it wished to remain in its headquarters on city-owned land. Failure to do so would require the chapter to pay $200,000 a year "fair-market rent" instead of the yearly lease of one dollar. The city told the Scouts that its policy of discrimination against homosexuals and atheists violated the city's antidiscrimination fair-practices law. The local council maintained it used a "don't ask, don't tell" practice but cannot change the policies without violating its charter from the national organization (Pynes 2009; Slobodzian 2007; Urbina 2007). The Cradle of Liberty Council filed a federal lawsuit to stay in the city-owned space. The lawsuit accused the city of censorship for targeting the Scouts but maintaining free or nominal leases with other groups that limit membership, such as the Baptist and Roman Catholic church groups and the Colonial Dames of America (Dale 2008; Hinkelman 2008; Pynes 2009, 2011; Slobodzian 2008).

When confronted with sexual-orientation discrimination, nonprofit managers find themselves in a complex legal environment. No federal legislation has been passed defining a national standard; thus, nonprofit managers face a patchwork of state and local laws, executive orders, and judicial and commission decisions barring such discrimination (Hostetler and Pynes 2000a, 2000b).

## Volunteer Management

Most nonprofits depend on volunteers. Volunteers serve as board members (chapter 3) and also perform other tasks that assist employees in meeting their agency's mission. Some grassroots or community-based, 501(c)(4) nonprofits such as the League of Women Voters (LWV) affiliates have only volunteers and members, while other 501(c)(3) nonprofits such as Big Brothers–Big Sisters have professional staff but depend heavily on volunteers to assist in delivering their programs. According to the Corporation for National and Community Service, the number of volunteers increased in 2009 to nearly 27 percent of the U.S. populations, or 63.4 million volunteers, who contributed 8.1 billion hours of service valued at approximately $169 billion (Corporation for National and Community Service 2010).

The increase in job loss among professionals has often been credited with an increase in volunteer activities. Professionals such as lawyers, accountants, and individuals who speak multiple languages have been willing to donate their talents to nonprofits while they seek employment. As a result of these workforce changes, many agencies have become more strategic in their volunteer recruitment strategies to reach individuals whose interests and skills are likely to match the needs of the nonprofit.

To recruit volunteers, many nonprofits have rethought the assignments they give to them in terms of time, location, and length of commitment. Many nonprofits have established volunteer banks where they can be assigned to projects that do not require a long-term commitment to the agency or fixed hours each week. Internet volunteering is a way for individuals to fit volunteering into their busy and often unpredictable schedules. It has been used to conduct research on the Web, track relevant legislation, give specialist advice, design a website or newsletter, create databases, and provide translation, as well as give e-mail mentoring (Murray and Harrison 2005).

**Leadership and Diversity Challenges**

Despite reduced budgets, nonprofits foresee a need to fill 24,000 vacant or new roles in areas like finance and fund-raising, amid increasing management complexity and baby boomer retirements (Bridgespan Group 2009). This is consistent with earlier reports of a nonprofit leadership void between 2010 and 2020 (Adams 2006; Hall 2006; Halpern 2006; Kunreuther 2005; Teegarden 2004). *Ready to Lead? Next Generation Leaders Speak Out* found there are a significant number of younger people willing to become nonprofit executives, but they are not ready to lead at this time (Cornelius et al. 2008).

The lack of leadership talent has resulted in many nonprofits' hiring interim executives who can provide temporary leadership while the board searches for the right candidate (Berkshire 2010). Greenlights for Nonprofit Success is a 501(c)(3) that provides Central Texas nonprofits with guidance on their management and governance issues. In 2008 it established an interim executive director program that provides temporary executives to run charities until a permanent leader can be found. It has a pool of former executive directors from which nonprofits can choose. The average stay is four to six months, and the interim executives deal with managing employees, overseeing programs, and handling budgets. The program was initiated because a survey conducted in 2007 indicated that 67 percent of 227 local nonprofits thought their executive directors would leave by 2012 (Ball 2010).

When recruiting for new executives, staff, and volunteers, nonprofits need to take into account the changing demographics of American society showing an increase in the number of employees who are women, members of ethnic and racial minorities, persons with disabilities, and from different generations with different knowledge, skills, abilities, and other characteristics (KSAOCs). Nonprofits should be engaged in workforce and succession planning, as well as developing strategies for sharing knowledge and experience.

Workforces that are representative of the constituents they serve will also be more successful in expanding their constituent and customer base and will be poised to capture new markets. For example, membership in the Boy Scouts of America has declined over the last ten years by 16 percent to 2.8 million. Most Scouts are white boys. Robert Mazzuca, chief executive of the Boy Scouts, recognizes the need to become more diverse, making a push among Hispanics. "We used to just translate our material into Spanish words, not linking them to things that are meaningful to Hispanics," Mazzuca said. Focus groups indicated that Hispanics regard the Boy Scouts as "elite and unattainable" (cited in Seelye 2010). The demographic group that has drawn the most attention in the Scouts is young girls. Girls are eligible to join the Boy Scouts once they have completed eighth grade. They can become members of the Boy Scouts' Venturing program, where many of the leaders are women. To increase membership in the Boy Scouts, one recommendation is to allow preteen girls to join and is presently being discussed. As the examples in the beginning of this chapter indicate, women and minorities are underrepresented in the top development positions at major nonprofits. This situation has been attributed to boards of directors' lack of commitment to diversity (Joslyn 2010), which will need to change if nonprofits plan on staying relevant and providing needed services and programs. Organizations that promote diversity will be able to attract and retain the best employees.

## Conclusion

New cultural and social changes are affecting nonprofits. Not only have nonprofit workforces become more demographically diverse but the values of employees have also changed. If nonprofits are going to be able to attract qualified employees and volunteers, they need to be flexible and have progressive HRM policies and programs in place. To accommodate the changing workforce, nonprofits should promote a greater awareness of diversity issues and cultural differences. It is also important that they audit their human resources functions to ensure that they are free from bias. Nonprofits must not only be innovative in how they treat and reward their employees and volunteers, but also be creative in how they recruit employees and volunteers.

## Case 7.1. Looking for Minority Board Members

The Minority Board Member Pipeline Initiative was founded in Cleveland, Ohio, by six black professionals to help match minority professionals with nonprofit boards. Randell McShepard, one of the founders of the initiative and vice president at RPM International, found himself fielding requests from twenty-two nonprofits asking him to serve on their board of directors. He recognized that the invitations underscore that nonprofits are not looking far enough to tap into the talents of minority professionals in the community. His experience is accurate. The Urban Institute's survey of more than 5,000 charities (cited in chapter 3) found that 86 percent of board members are white, 7 percent are black, and 3.5 are Hispanic.

Elizabeth Hosler Voudouris, executive vice president of Business Unlimited, commented that boards need to be diverse to guide nonprofits, because in many cases the stakeholders that the organizations serve represent diverse races, ethnicities, cultures, and socioeconomic backgrounds, and it is critical to have the perspectives of minority board members.

Business Volunteers Unlimited and the Minority Pipeline cosponsor seminars for minority professionals serving on boards. The Minority Pipeline recruits minority professionals for its seminars through organizations such as the Urban League Young Professionals and the Cleveland Chapter of the National Society of Hispanic MBAs.

*Source:* McClelland-Copeland 2008.

## Case 7.2. Do Environmental Nonprofits Need More Diversity?

When Jerome C. Ringo joined the board of the National Wildlife Foundation in 1995, he was the only African American at the meeting. In 2009, he still is usually the only environmentalist in the room who is not white. In 1990, leaders of civil rights and minority groups wrote an open letter that accused the ten biggest environmental organizations of "racist" hiring practices. Richard Moore, one of the letter's signers, said the public indictment was set off by several cases in which the groups had pushed for protection of lands at the expense of minority communities.

Groups like the National Resources Defense Council have formed partnerships with smaller environmental groups that emerged in the 1980s and '90s to represent the interests of low-income and minority constituencies.

Roger Rivera, president of the National Hispanic Environmental Council, an advocacy group in Washington that promotes environmental careers among Latino students, said that for more than a year he had been attending meetings of the Green Group, a loose association of about three dozen environmental organizations, as an observer. He was invited to join in January 2009, after the election of the first black president of the United States.

*Source:* Navarro 2009.

## References

Adams, T. (2006). *Staying engaged, stepping up: Succession planning and executive transition management for nonprofit boards of directors. Executive Transitions Monograph Series*, vol. 5. Baltimore: Annie E. Casey Foundation. www.aecf.org/upload/publicationfiles/stayingengaged,steppingup.pdf.

American Civil Liberties Union (2010). White House must reform faith-based initiative, says ACLU. February 5.www.aclu.org/religion-belief/white-house-must-reform-faith-based-initiative-says-aclu.

Ball, A. (2010). Interim executive directors help out. *Austin Statesman,* August 22. www.statesman.com/news/local/interim-executive-directors-help-out-871977.html.

Berkshire, J.C. (2010). As boomers retire, more nonprofit groups hire interim leaders. *Chronicle of Philanthropy,* June 13, 23, 27.

*Board of Directors, Rotary International v. Rotary Club of Duarte* (1987). 481 U.S. 537, 544, 107 S.Ct. 1940, 1945, 95 L. ED. 2d 474, 483–84.

Bogan, J. (2010). Gay member of Catholic nonprofit told he cannot be president because he's gay. *St. Louis Post-Dispatch,* April 14. www.stltoday.com/lifestyles/faith-and-values/article_3f3a0935–840d-5494-bcc1-afbaffb07b14.html.

*Boy Scouts of America and Monmouth Council, et al., Petitioners, v. James Dale* (2000). 530 U.S. 640.

Bridgespan Group (2009). Nonprofits seek to fill 24,000 leadership roles in downturn. April 20. www.bridgespan.org/LearningCenter/ResourceDetail.aspx?id=3830.

Civil Rights Act of 1964, Title VII, Sec. 70, Section 702, 703(e)(2).

Cornelius, M., P. Corvington, and A. Ruesga (2008). Ready to lead? Next generation leaders speak out. National study. Baltimore: CompassPoint Nonprofit Services, Annie E. Casey Foundation, the Meyer Foundation and Idealist.org. www.meyerfoundation.org/newsroom/meyer_publications/ready_to_lead.

*Corporation of the Presiding Bishop of the Church of Jesus Christ of Latter-Day Saints et al. v. Amos et al.* (1987). 483 U.S. 327.

Corporation for National and Community Service, Office of Research and Policy Development (2010). Volunteering in America 2010: National, state, and city information, Washington, DC, June.

*Coulee Catholic Schools v. Labor and Industry Review Commission, Department of Workforce Development and Wendy Ostlund* (2009). July 21. 312 Wis. 2d 331, 752 N.W. 2d 341.

Dale, M. (2008). Scouts sue after Philly demands rent or new policy. Associated Press. May 27. http:www.msnbc.msn.com/id/24843065/ns/us_wws-life.

*Dale v. Boy Scouts of America and Monmouth Council Boy Scouts* (1998). A-24279573, N.J. Supreme Court.

*Dale v. Boy Scouts of America and Monmouth Council Boy Scouts* (1999). A-195/1997, N.J. Supreme Court.

De Vita, C.J. (1999). Nonprofits and devolution: What do we know? In *Nonprofits and government: Collaboration and conflict,* ed. E.T. Boris and C.E. Steuerle, 213–33. Washington, DC: Urban Institute Press.

Flandez, R. (2010). Religious charities gear up to fight federal hiring proposal. *Chronicle of Philanthropy,* September 9, 12.

Gorenstein, N. (2010). Jury says Philly can't evict Boy Scouts for anti-gay policy. *Philadelphia Inquirer,* June 24. wwww. articles.philly.com.2010–06–24/news/24962341_1_city-solicitor-shelley-smith-anti-gay-policy-liberty-council, accessed March 21, 2011.

Gossett, C.W., and J.E. Pynes (2003). The expansion of "charitable choice" and "faith-based initiatives"—HRM implications for nonprofit organizations. *Review of Public Personnel Administration,* 23(2), 154–68.

Hall, H. (2006). Smooth transitions: Experts offer tips on hiring new leaders. *Chronicle of Philanthropy,* 17(6), 11.

Halpern, R.P. (2006). *Workforce issues in the nonprofit sector: Generational leadership change and diversity.* Kansas City, MO: American Humanics.

Hinkelman, M. (2008). Scouts sue the city to stay in $1 HQ. *Philadelphia Daily News,* May 28.

Hostetler, D.W., and J.E. Pynes (2000a). Sexual orientation discrimination and how it challenges nonprofit managers. *Nonprofit Management & Leadership,* 11(1), 49–63.

———. (2000b). Commentary: Sexual orientation discrimination and how it challenges nonprofit managers. *Nonprofit Management & Leadership,* 11(2), 235–37.

*Hurley v. Irish American Gay Group of Boston* (1995). U.S. No. 94–749 (1995).

Joslyn, H. (2010). Women and minorities lag in appointments to top fund-raising jobs. *Chronicle of Philanthropy,* September 9, D-3, D-4.

Kunreuther, F. (2005). *Up next: Generation change and the leadership of nonprofit organizations.* Baltimore: Annie E. Casey Foundation.

Lee, D.A. (2010). Tarpon Springs allows hiring at hospital based on religion. *St. Petersburg Times,* August 18, 7B.

*Lown v. the Salvation Army, Inc.; Commission, New York City Administration for Children Services and others* (2005). 04 Civ. 1562 (SHS) September 30.

Lupu, I.C., and R.W. Tuttle (2005). Legal update: *Lown v. the Salvation Army, Inc.; Commission, New York City Administration for Children Services and others.* www.religionandsocialpolicy.org/legal/legal_update_display.cfm?id=38.

McClelland-Copeland, A. (2008). Minorities say nonprofit boards not looking deep enough among their numbers. As cited in *Philanthropy News Digest* (A Service of the Foundation Center) "Cleveland Group Work to Boost Diversity of Nonprofit Boards" July 4, 2008. http://foundationcenter.org/pnd/news/story.jhtml?id=219900066.

Morning, J., and A. Tansimore (2010). At grant-making organizations, diversity needs to start at the top. *Chronicle of Philanthropy,* September 9, D-10.

Murray, V., and Y. Harrison (2005). Virtual volunteering. *Emerging areas of volunteering,* ARNOVA Occasional Paper Series 1 (2), 31–47.

Navarro, M. (2009). In environmental push, looking to add diversity. *New York Times,* March 10, A13.

*Pedreira v. Kentucky Baptist Homes for Children* (2001). U.S. District Court for the Western District of Kentucky, July 23. No. CIV.A.3:00CV-210-S.

*Petruska v. Gannon University* (2006a). 3rd Cir. 5/24/2006.

———. (2006b). 3rd Cir. 6/20/2006.

Posner, S. (2010). Religious leaders pressure Congress to support religious discrimination. *Religion Dispatches Magazine.* August 26. www.religiondispatches.org/dispatches/sarahposner/3215/religious_leaders_pressure_congress_to_support_religious_discrimination/.

Pynes, J.E. (2009). *Human resources management for public and nonprofit organizations: A strategic approach.* 3rd ed. San Francisco: Jossey-Bass.

———. (2011). Human resource management challenges in nonprofit organizations. In *Public personnel management: Current concerns, future challenges* (5th ed.), ed. Norma M. Riccucci, 196–212. New York: Longman.

Seelye, K.Q. (2010). Boy Scouts seek a way to rebuild ranks. *New York Times,* June 30, A11.

Slobodzian, J.A. (2007). Scouts ignore gay-policy deadline. *Philadelphia Inquirer*, December 4. www.philly.com/inquirer/local/philadelphia/20071204_Scouts_ ignore_gay-policy_deadline.html.
———. (2008). Boy Scouts sue city in building dispute. *Philadelphia Inquirer*, May 24.
Strom, S. (2010). Religion-based groups protest restrictions in bill. *New York Times*, August 25, A18.
Teegarden, P.H. (2004). *Nonprofit executive leadership and transitions survey 2004*. Baltimore: Annie E. Casey Foundation.
*Tomic v. Catholic Diocese of Peoria* (2006). 442 F.3d 1036.
United Press International (UPI) (2010). Jury: Phila. may not evict Scouts. June 23. www.upi.com/Top_News/US/2010/06/23/Jury-Phila-may-not-evict-scouts/ UPI-24231277351778/.
Urbina, I. (2007). Boy Scouts lose Philadelphia lease in gay-rights fight. *New York Times*, December 6. www.nytimes.com/2007/12/06/us/06scouts.html.
Wallsten, P. (2010). Keeping faith, courting conservatives. *Wall Street Journal*, February 4. http://online.wsj.com/article/SB10001424052748703357104575045623785996294.html.

# 8

# Advocacy and Lobbying

## Making Your Voices Heard

*Congress shall make no law respecting an establishment of religion, or prohibiting the free exercise thereof; or abridging the freedom of speech, or of the press; or the right of the people peaceably to assemble, and to petition the Government for a redress of grievances.*

—First Amendment to the U.S. Constitution

Nonprofits have been instrumental in provoking some of the most important social changes in this country though a combination of research, public education, advocacy, legislation, and litigation. Nonprofits sometimes work in coalitions, sometimes in collaboration with government and business interests, and sometimes in conflict with them and other nonprofits (Boris 2006).

Civil rights, women's rights, environmental movements, domestic violence, providing services to persons with HIV, advocating for services for individuals with physical and mental disabilities, and advancing justice for lesbian, bisexual, gay, and transgendered (LBGT) individuals are just a few examples of where nonprofits called attention to issues and provided leadership on those issues ahead of government. The adversarial and advocacy roles played by nonprofits have been critical in the development of who we are as a society and what we value (O'Connell 1999; Salamon 2002; Young 2006).

Young (2006) identifies three roles that nonprofits play in society. They provide a *complementary role,* helping to deliver public goods that are largely financed by government; a *supplementary role*, focusing on the needs that are unsatisfied by government, overlooked or emerging, or that do not have enough support from voters at a particular time; and an *adversarial role*, prompting the government to make changes in public policy and maintain accountability to the public. He notes that these roles do not function in isolation—a nonprofit agency such as Planned Parenthood can deliver government services funded by public contracts, provide some services funded by private donations, as well as focus on advocacy or challenging public policy.

Also recognizing the important role played by nonprofits in influencing public policy, Salamon (2002, 10) believes that advocacy is the most important role undertaken by nonprofits. He states the following:

> In addition to delivering services, nonprofit organizations also contribute to national life by identifying unaddressed problems and bringing them to public attention, by protecting basic human rights, and by giving voice to a wide assortment of social, political, environmental, ethnic, and community interests and concerns. Most of the social movements that have animated American life over the past century or more operated in and through the nonprofit sector. Included here are the antislavery, women's suffrage, populist, progressive, civil rights, environmental, antiwar, women's, gay rights, and conservative movements. The nonprofit sector has thus operated as a critical social safety valve, permitting aggrieved groups to bring their concerns to broader public attention and to rally support to improve their circumstances. This advocacy role may, in fact, be more important to the nation's social health than the service functions the sector also performs.

This chapter will address the following topics:

- What is the difference between advocacy and lobbying?
- What role does lobbying play in the public policy process?
- How can advocacy efforts influence public policy?
- What skills are needed by nonprofit managers to be effective in their advocacy efforts?

## Are 501(c)(3) Public Charity Nonprofits Active Enough?

Two recent research projects have investigated the factors that motivate nonprofits to engage in public policy matters. The Strengthening Nonprofit Advocacy Project (SNAP) sampled public charities to find out the nature and extent of advocacy activities. The project was supported by a number of organizations and foundations: the Aspen Institute's Nonprofit

Sector Research Fund, Atlantic Philanthropies, the Nathan Cummings Foundation, the Ford Foundation, the Robert Wood Johnson Foundation, the David and Lucile Packard Foundation, the Surdna Foundation, research teams from OMB Watch, Tufts University, and the Center for Lobbying in the Public Interest, as well as advisers from individual nonprofits across the country.

The SNAP Project (Bass et al. 2007, 17–18) found that the frequency of policy participation by nonprofits is inconsistent and generally low; roughly three of four nonprofits say they have engaged at least once in key types of public policy activity, from direct grassroots lobbying to testifying at a legislative or administrative hearing. Nonprofits say that public policy participation is essential to carrying out their mission, but that engaging in policy activities detracts them from other administrative tasks. Even when nonprofits engage in public policy matters, they do not think of themselves as influencing public policy. Generally health and environmental groups report the most involvement in public policy, arts and recreation the least.

Nonprofits differ widely in how they interpret words that are used to describe public participation, particularly the words "lobbying," "advocacy," and "educating." These results are similar to those identified by the Listening Post Project, a joint project of the Center for Civil Society Studies at the Johns Hopkins Institute for Policy Studies in cooperation with the Alliance for Children and Families, the Alliance for Nonprofit Management, the American Association of Homes and Services for the Aging, the American Association of Museums, Lutheran Services in America, the National Council of Nonprofit Associations, and the United Neighborhood Centers of America (Salamon et al. 2008).

SNAP and the Listening Post Project found that limited resources are devoted to lobbying or advocacy activities; that chief executives are typically the employees most involved in policy issues; that the principal targets of policy activities are local and state governments; that the most common reasons cited for a lack of advocacy or lobbying activities were the lack of staff time, lack of staff skills, and a reliance on coalitions and intermediaries to engage in lobbying and advocacy efforts. Additional factors relating to advocacy or lobbying activities were organizational size and age, receipt of public funds, board support, and knowledge of the law. The SNAP Project (Bass et al. 2007) found that a number of nonprofits did not understand the regulations in regard to advocacy and lobbying, feared upsetting government and foundation funders, and also feared risking their tax exemption. The Listening Post Project found few nonprofits citing these concerns (Salamon et al. 2008).

## What Are the Differences Between Advocacy and Lobbying Activities?

*Advocacy* is considered to be actions taken in support of a cause or idea. It may include providing information, distributing information, or holding events to dramatize an issue or the effects of a problem on individuals or a community. Advocacy is the right of every individual or organization and may be practiced without limits. Free speech, the right to assemble, and the right to petition government for a redress of grievances are advocacy activities.

*Lobbying* is considered to be actions taken to support or oppose specific legislation at the national, state, or local level. Contacting members of Congress, state legislators, or city or county commissioners to request sponsorship or votes in favor or against specific legislation is considered lobbying. It typically does not include contacting members of the executive branch, unless those individuals are in positions to influence legislation. The IRS defines lobbying as any attempt to influence legislation. Any lobbying a nonprofit conducts must be "insubstantial" in relationship to its overall efforts to achieve its charitable mission.

> In general, no organization may qualify for section 501(c)(3) status if a substantial part of its activities is attempting to influence legislation (commonly known as *lobbying*). A 501(c)(3) organization may engage in some lobbying, but too much lobbying activity risks loss of tax exempt status.
> *Legislation* includes action by Congress, any state legislature, any local council, or similar governing body, with respect to acts, bills, resolutions, or similar items (such as legislative confirmation of appointive office), or by the public in referendum, ballot initiative, constitutional amendment, or similar procedure. It does not include actions by executive, judicial, or administrative bodies.
> An organization will be regarded as attempting to influence legislation if it contacts, or urges the public to contact, members or employees of a legislative body for the purpose of proposing, supporting, or opposing legislation, or if the organization advocates the adoption or rejection of legislation.
> Organizations may, however, involve themselves in issues of public

policy without the activity being considered as lobbying. For example, organizations may conduct educational meetings, prepare and distribute educational materials, or otherwise consider public policy issues in an educational manner without jeopardizing their tax-exempt status. (IRS 2010a)

Independent sector nonprofits [501(c)(3) and 501(c)(4)] are permitted to engage in advocacy and lobbying activities. They must, however, comply with Internal Revenue Code limitations on their lobbying activity and are prohibited from participating in political campaigns or endorsing or opposing candidates running for elective office. Nor can they publish or distribute statements or printed materials in favor or against a specific candidate.

Public charity 501(c)(3) nonprofits are tax-exempt and able to receive tax-deductible contributions, which are viewed as public subsidies provided to them. The purpose of the subsidies is to support an organization's charitable activities, and the law requires that its resources be used to pursue those purposes as its primary activity. If there were no subsidies for nonprofits, government could spend more on various programs or create other subsidies. Regulation of lobbying is grounded in the belief that the subsidy granted through the tax code gives the government the authority to restrict such behavior. The U.S. Supreme Court held in *Regan v. Taxation with Representation* (1983) 461 U.S. 540 (1983) that "deductible contributions are similar to cash grants from the government." The Court held that in writing its tax laws, Congress had clearly made a conscious decision not to subsidize lobbying by nonprofits.

## What Is Meant by Substantial and Insubstantial Lobbying?

Prior to 1976, the meanings of insubstantial and substantial were unclear. The Internal Revenue Service (IRS) never defined the terms but looked at each situation on a case-by-case basis. One of the problems was that the substantial-part test looked not only at how much a nonprofit spent on lobbying activity but also at how much time and effort was devoted to the activity. The courts were inconsistent in the definitions; some courts held that nonprofits were safe if they spent less than 5 percent of their budget on lobbying, but other courts said such an arbitrary standard was not appropriate. Nonprofits were confronted with inconsistent messages;

they were unsure how much time and how much money devoted to lobbying would be considered by the IRS to be a substantial part of their activities. As a result, some nonprofits refrained from lobbying rather than risk losing their tax-exempt status.

In 1976, Congress passed Public Law 94–455, which sought to clarify the situation, and in 1990, the IRS issued sections 4911 and 501 of the Internal Revenue Code, describing how the law would be implemented. Since then, nonprofits have two options, the *Substantial-Part Test* or the *501(h) Expenditure Test*.

The substantial-part test still remains an imprecise standard. The IRS definition is provided below.

> Whether an organization's attempts to influence legislation, i.e., *lobbying*, constitute a substantial part of its overall activities is determined on the basis of all the pertinent facts and circumstances in each case. The IRS considers a variety of factors, including the time devoted (by both compensated and volunteer workers) and the expenditures devoted by the organization to the activity, when determining whether the lobbying activity is substantial.
>
> Under the substantial part test, an organization that conducts excessive lobbying in any taxable year may lose its tax-exempt status, resulting in all of its income being subject to tax. In addition, section 501(c)(3) organizations that lose their tax-exempt status due to excessive lobbying, other than churches and private foundations, are subject to an excise tax equal to five percent of their lobbying expenditures for the year in which they cease to qualify for exemption.
>
> Further, a tax equal to five percent of the lobbying expenditures for the year may be imposed against organization managers, jointly and severally, who agree to the making of such expenditures knowing that the expenditures would likely result in the loss of tax-exempt status.
>
> Private foundations are subject to a different set of taxes on their lobbying expenditures; churches are not subject to excise taxes on excessive lobbying. (IRS 2010b)

The 501(h) Expenditure Test provided by the 1976 law and subsequent IRS regulations require nonprofits to file IRS Form 5768, electing to be covered by the specific expenditure guidelines under 501(h) of the Internal Revenue Code. This option does not consider the amount of time or effort devoted to lobbying; instead it is based entirely on how much the organization spends on lobbying activity as a percentage of its total budget. Lobbying activities that do not involve expenditures are not limited. For example, if volunteers call on legislators, those efforts do not count unless the nonprofit spends money to support the activity. If the nonprofit reimburses the volunteers for their transportation to the meeting, that expense would need to be included in its lobbying expense, but the volunteers' time would not. The 501(h) option also presents fewer risks for nonprofits than does the substantial-part test. Nonprofits that may exceed their spending limits will not lose their tax exemption unless they exceed them by at least 150 percent averaged over a four-year period. And there are no penalties imposed on individual managers of an organization that exceeds its limits.

## 501(c)(3) Lobbying

If a 501(c)(3) elects to take the 501(h) exemption, it is governed by the following rules. The total lobbying expenditure limits under the 501(h) are

- 20 percent of the first $500,000 of exempt purpose expenditures,
  +
- 15 percent of the next $500,000 of exempt purpose expenditures,
  +
- 10 percent of the next $500,000 of exempt purpose expenditures,
  +
- 5 percent of the remaining exempt purpose expenditures up to a total cap of $1 million.

Exempt purpose expenditures are all payments made in one year, except those on investment-managed unrelated businesses and certain fundraising expenses. The spending limits are stated as a percentage of the nonprofit's total expenditures (on exempt activities) on a sliding scale, depending on the size of the organization.

Under the 501(h) election, the IRS distinguishes between *direct* and *grassroots* lobbying. *Direct lobbying* "refers to communication that your organization has with legislators or government officials who participate in the formulation of legislation, and with its own members" (Smucker 2005, 240). Thus, the definition does not include communication with officials of the executive branch of government or communication that just provides information without expressing an opinion for or against the legislation. Direct lobbying is when nonprofits state their positions on specific legislation to legislators and other government employees who participate in the formulation of legislation, or urge their members to do so. To count as direct lobbying, the nonprofit must refer to specific legislation and express a view on it. A call to protect children from abuse is not direct lobbying.

*Grassroots lobbying* refers to "any attempt to influence legislation by affecting the opinion of the general public and that asks individuals to take action" (Smucker 2005, 240). Grassroots lobbying is when nonprofits state their position on specific legislation to the general public and ask them to contact legislators or other government employees who participate in the formulation of legislation. If they do not include a call to action in their communication to the general public, it is not lobbying. Informing the public about a specific bill, but not stating a position for or against, is not grassroots lobbying. Urging its own members to lobby would be considered direct lobbying, not grassroots lobbying.

The distinction between direct and grassroots lobbying is important under the 501(h) election because the 1976 Lobby Law specifies different expenditure limits for grassroots and direct lobbying activity. The expenditures on grassroots lobbying should only be one-fourth of that on direct lobbying. If an organization's annual permissible lobbying expenditures are $100,000, it can spend only $25,000 on grassroots lobbying; it can spend the remaining $75,000, or the full $100,000, on direct lobbying.

Not all activity, even though it may impact an elected official's vote, is considered lobbying. Exclusions from the term "influencing legislation" include *self-defense* communication on any legislation that would affect an organization's existence, powers and duties, tax-exempt status, or deductibility of contributions; providing *technical advice* to a governmental body in response to a written communication; *conducting nonpartisan analysis or research*—studying community problems and their potential solutions is considered nonpartisan if it is an independent and objective exposition of a particular subject matter that may advocate a particular position or viewpoint so long as there is a sufficiently full and fair exposition of pertinent facts to enable the public or an individual to form an independent opinion or conclusion.

*Communication with the organization's own members* with respect to legislation that is of direct interest to them is not lobbying, so long as the discussion does not address the merits of a specified legislative proposal and contains no call for action.

Communication with executive branch governmental officials or employees on *regulatory and administrative matters* is considered to be exempt.

*Efforts to educate and inform elected officials and the general public* about the general value and benefit of a nonprofit's programs, services, mission, projects, and so on, as long as they do not relate directly to, or urge specific action on, any given piece of legislation, are not lobbying. Keeping an elected official apprised of what the organization is doing or informing officials and the public about the positive results and benefit to society of a given program or programs is not lobbying as long as the effort is not connected to urging specific action on specific legislation.

Charitable nonprofits must report their lobbying expenses on IRS Form 990. In addition, organizations that hire professional lobbyists and spend more than $24,500 (indexed for inflation) on lobbying at the federal level must meet the requirements of the Lobbying Disclosure Act of 1995. This requires that they register and report their lobbying expenditures to Congress on a semiannual basis.

*Religious organizations* (churches, synagogues, mosques, and all other houses of worship) are 501(c)(3) organizations and can lobby as long as lobbying is an insubstantial part of their overall activities. Unlike other public charities, religious organizations cannot elect to measure their lobbying under the 501(h) expenditure test. This is because when Congress passed section 501(h) of the Internal Revenue Code in 1976, religious organizations asked not to be subject to it, so they are subject to the "insubstantial part" test. Religious organizations risk losing their tax exempt status if their lobbying activities are substantial (Alliance for Justice 2007; Dessingue 2004).

## 501(c)(4) Nonprofits and Lobbying

Social Welfare 501(c)(4) nonprofits have fewer tax law restrictions than 501(c)(3) nonprofits in regard to political activity. They can engage in unlimited lobbying and can encourage their members to support particular candidates for public office. They can engage in all of the nonpartisan voter education activity that a 501(c)(3) can, but also in unlimited lobbying that includes ballot measures; can endorse federal candidates for office to its membership and share the endorsement with its press list; can expressly advocate for a federal candidate's election or defeat when communicating with its membership; and can create an affiliated 527 political organization. Social Welfare 501(c)(4) nonprofits cannot communicate with the general public that they endorse a federal candidate, nor can they coordinate communications with a federal candidate or party; they cannot make cash or in-kind contributions to federal candidates, nor engage in electoral activity as their primary activity (Alliance for Justice 2007).

### *Individuals Can Be Politically Engaged!*

Individual members, board officers, staff, volunteers, or other supporters of the mission or specific programs of nonprofit agencies are permitted to support, work for, endorse, or contribute money to the campaigns of individuals running for elective office. If they are acting as individuals only and not as a representative of a nonprofit, they are not banned from opposing or supporting candidates. As long as individuals do not claim to be speaking on behalf of the nonprofits with which they are affiliated, or use the nonprofit's means of communications to make known their stand, it is their constitutional right to lobby and support or oppose candidates (Hessenius 2007, 62).

### *Private Foundations*

Private foundations may not endorse or oppose legislation. They may provide technical advice to a legislature if asked to do so, provide non-partisan analyses and studies, and lobby in self-defense. Foundations are also barred from participating in political campaigns. They can support nonpartisan activities such as candidate forums and get-out-the-vote drives, but they face strict regulations of their participation in voter registration drives (Independent Sector 2010).

### *Political Action Committees*

Political action committees (PACs) are allowed to support, endorse, and make contribution to the campaigns of candidates for office, which is prohibited for 501(c)(3) or 501(c)(4) organizations. But 501(c)(3) or 501(c)(4) nonprofits can create a PAC, which can be a separate fund set up by a 501(c) organization. The PAC cannot solicit or accept funds from the nonprofit, so it cannot operate with funds from the parent nonprofit's general budget. It can appeal to its members to contribute funds to its PAC, but those contributions will not be tax-deductible for the donor. There are limits on how much individuals can contribute to a PAC, on how much a PAC can contribute to a given candidate, and on the total that can be given to all candidates. To avoid legal complications, accurate books and records of where the money came from must be maintained.

### *Section 527 Political Organizations*

Section 527 political organizations are a type of tax-exempt organization named after a section of the United States tax code—26 U.S.C. § 527. A 527 group is created primarily to *influence* the nomination, election, appointment, or defeat of candidates for public office. Because 527 political organizations do not make expenditures to directly advocate the election or defeat of any candidate for federal elective office, they avoid regulation by the Federal Election Commission. Many 527 political organizations are run by interest groups and are used to raise money to spend on issue advocacy and voter mobilization outside of the restrictions on PACs.

A 527 political organization is permitted to accept contributions of any amount from any source. However, it is required to make regular reports to the IRS of its funding and expenditures. It can spend money to elect or defeat candidates, but it cannot give money to the candidate directly or be directly associated with the campaign. Section 527 organizations may engage in issue advocacy, including educating the public about officeholders voting records, positions on issues, views, and qualifications, and in voter registration drives.

### Should 501(c)(3) Nonprofits Fear Losing Their Tax Exemptions?

Over the years there have been efforts to make it more difficult for public charities to be actively involved in advocacy and lobbying activities. The Sierra Club's losing its 501(c)(3) tax exemption has been used as a prominent example. In 1966 Congress considered building dams on the Colorado River to turn the Grand Canyon into a lake. To oppose the construction of dams, the Sierra Club took out newspaper advertisements criticizing Congress. Part of the advertisement had a form readers could clip and send to the congressional subcommittee's chair in protest. As a result, the Sierra Club came under investigation for possibly violating its prohibition against substantial lobbying. The Sierra Club's 501(c)(3) tax-exempt status was revoked by the IRS, and it became a 501(c)(4) nonprofit (Bass et al. 2007; Berry and Arons 2005).

Brian O'Connell (1999) shares his experience as the national director of the Mental Health Association (MHA). After working to increase appropriations from Congress for mental health research, training, and community treatment and finding that President Nixon would not release the funds, MHA sued the president, with the case eventually ending up in the U.S. Supreme Court, which sided with MHA. After the Court victories, MHA affiliates were subject to IRS financial and program audits as punishment.

Another attempt to influence the activities of nonprofits took place during the Reagan administration. The Office of Management and Budget (OMB) Circular A-122, "Cost Principles for Nonprofits," sets forth accounting rules for cost sharing and how much overhead could be charged to federal grants. It prevents nonprofits that receive federal money from using that money to lobby government. During the Reagan administration, there was an attempt to amend the guidelines to forbid any federal dollars used in cost sharing from federal grants for facilities and staff involved in lobbying (Berry and Arons 2005; O'Connell 1999). The definition of lobbying was expanded to include attempts to influence government decisions at any branch of government. If approved, public charities receiving federal dollars would not be able to engage in advocacy and would have been required to start a separate nonprofit to do lobbying. The changes were never made, because while it was easy to criticize advocacy groups such as the American Civil Liberties Union (ACLU) and the Sierra Club, members of Congress had a hard time answering their constituents' concerns as to why nonprofits such as the United Way, Meals on Wheels, and other community agencies they were involved with were being punished. James Baker, President Reagan's chief of staff, instructed the Office of Management and Budget (OMB) to withdraw the rules (Berry and Arons 2005, 83). There were other attempts. In 1995, the House of Representatives passed a rider to an appropriations bill sponsored by Representative Ernest Istook (R-Oklahoma), David McIntosh (R-Indiana), and Robert Ehrlich (R-Maryland) that was a rehash of OMB Circular A-122 to fight to "defund the left," but it went further. The Istook Amendment would have expanded the existing prohibition on using federal funds for lobbying to include "political advocacy" activities, which were broadly defined. It would have included attempts to influence the executive and judicial branches of government. It would have barred charities from receiving federal grants if they spent 5 percent or more of their private funds for "political advocacy" activities. And it would have barred associating with other entities that use 15 percent or more of their money for advocacy activities. The amendment proposed new enforcement procedures, including licensing private citizens to find groups in violation of the various provisions of the bill. Anyone could have brought a lawsuit against a grantee for up to ten years after the violation. Organizations found out of compliance with the bill could have been fined $5,000 to $10,000 plus three times the value of the grant. The private citizens citing violations could have collected up to 25 percent of the recovery dollars. The Istook Amendment also only applied to federal grantees, not to contractors receiving federal funds. Many thought it was unfair. An amendment offered by a Democrat in the House of Representative to apply the Istook Amendment to contractors was defeated, further demonstrating that this issue was an attack on nonprofit federal grantees. Linked together by the Let America Speak coalition, charities worked to stop the Istook Amendment (Bass et al. 2007, 96).

## What About 501(c)(4)s?

Senator Alan Simpson (R-Wyoming) launched his own investigation of lobbying by the American Association of Retired Persons (AARP). He argued that 501(c)(4) organizations should not be allowed to receive federal grant money because they do not face the same lobbying limits as 501(c)(3) charities. Simpson, joined by Senator Carl Levin (D-Michigan) supported a provision that would prohibit 501(c)(4) nonprofits that lobby from receiving federal grant funds. However, the provision allowed a 501(c)(4) to be affiliated with a 501(c)(3) that could receive money. This provision became law (Bass et al. 2007, 100).

Attempts continued to add advocacy restrictions in appropriation bills for the Veterans Administration, the Department of Housing and Urban Development, and the Environmental Protection Agency. The proposed legislation did not pass, but the result made many nonprofits understand that there were risks involved in advocacy and lobbying activities. Most recently, in March 2009, there was an attempt by Representative Virginia Fox (R-North Carolina) and Senator Jim DeMint (R-South Carolina) to include amendments to the Edward M. Kennedy Serve America Act that would disqualify organizations from participating in national service programs if they engaged in political or legislative advocacy, whether or not the activities were funded outside the context of a national service program. It would ban participation in national service programs by organizations "co-located" on the same premises as an organization that lobbies for charitable purposes. Volunteers under AmeriCorps would also be restricted even on their personal time from engaging in lobbying, petitions, protests, boycotts, or strikes, union organizing, and engaging in partisan political activities and voter registration drives. The version of the act passed by the Senate and signed by President Obama on April 21, 2009, contains restrictions on the types of activities for which national service positions can be used—preventing participants from engaging in voter registration drives or political or legislative advocacy, or providing abortion services—but the nonprofits are free to utilize their own funds to advocate for causes in which they believe.

It is not just progressive organizations that are concerned that some of the IRS's enforcement has inhibited nonprofits from engaging in advocacy activities; churches and conservative organizations have made that claim as well. Some want to change the law to permit nonprofits to become involved in partisan politics, while others argue that doing so would set a dangerous precedent and cause nonprofits to lose one of their most important qualities, their independence from government and elected officials (Goodstein 2008; Merriam 2008; OMB Watch 2008; Slevin 2008; Vitello 2008).

## How Nonprofit Coalitions Can Become Involved in Political Campaigns

Hessenius (2007, 53–56) demonstrates how nonprofit coalitions can support or oppose specific legislation, and support candidates for public office provided they create the structures required by law and adhere to the rules and regulations governing each. For a nonprofit coalition to avail itself of the full range of options to lobby, it needs to create four legal entities:

First is a new 501(c)(3) organization that will represent the coalition. Nonprofits can band together with other nonprofits within their field and form a new 501(c)(3) nonprofit organization to manage and direct the coalition's general advocacy efforts.

That organization can then form a new 501(c)(4). It can spend its income on lobbying, but cannot engage in candidate support or opposition directly or indirectly.

The 501(c)(4) organization can create a tax-exempt PAC and solicit donations. The PAC can provide financial support to candidates for office.

It can recruit new members from the general public, and the dues those new members pay can be used to support candidates for office within the rules governing PACs.

The 501(c)(4) can create a 527-organization fund, and solicit donations from the public. The money may be spent on supporting issues, which may include, indirectly, money spent to support or oppose a candidate in a federal election so long as there is no link or coordination whatsoever between the 527 fund and the campaign organization or any specific candidate.

## Technology and Advocacy

The development of information and communication technology (ICT) has changed the capacity of nonprofits to build coalitions and networks to advocate and initiate actions. Electronic advocacy refers to the use of ICT technology to influence the decision-making process, or to the use of technology in an effort to support policy change efforts (Hick and McNutt, 2002). *Traditional electronic advocacy* involves the use of television, radio, fax, and other similar types of technology. *Emergent electronic advocacy* uses Internet-based technologies such as Web pages, e-mail, discussion groups, news groups, listservs, chat rooms, online fund-raising, virtual communities, alternative news and information services, online petitions, online surveys, videoconferencing, banner ads, targeting and mapping software, and virtual civil disobedience (hacktivism) (FitzGerald and McNutt 1999). Some of the newer strategies include:

- *Community networking.* Community networks, or FreeNets, are locality-based systems designed to serve their immediate communities with ways to communicate and deliberate virtually. They also provide online services for their communities, including the ability to have civic discussion and debate as well as the opportunity for small organizations to have an online presence.
- *Electronic democracy or e-government.* Involves the creation of electronic town halls and similar forums for public debate. These are generally provided by local governments but can be sponsored by local nonprofit organizations. They provide a political free space for dealing with public issues.
- *Electronic government relations.* Includes predominantly legislative advocacy. Techniques include petitions, letter-writing campaigns, and similar efforts.

- *Virtual communities.* A community of people that exists only on-line; the individuals do not meet face to face. Online social action organizing aims at bringing communities, groups, and individuals together to redistribute power.
- *Civil disobedience.* It involves interfering with the operation of opponents' materials—or even stealing from their computers or destroying their technology. It has been referred to as hacktivism because it can include efforts to hack into an opponent's computer system.

These newer technologies either replace or augment activities that were previously done by other means. For example, e-mail action alerts are the electronic version of the flyers that grassroots organizers hand out on street corners or at rallies. The difference is that e-mail alerts reach more people instantly and cost nothing (Hick and McNutt 2002, 3–18).

In most cases the rules for advocacy, political behavior, and lobbying are the same if distributed through the ICT technologies. The Alliance for Justice has provided an interpretation of political and lobbying activities that nonprofits implement through the Internet. It can be obtained through its website at www.afj.org.

## Conclusion

Current research indicates that many nonprofits are not as active as they could be in influencing public policy. Barriers to policy participation include limited financial resources, a lack of understanding of the tax law and IRS regulations, and limited staff and volunteer skills. In many nonprofits, especially the smaller ones, staff and the executive director are already overextended (Bass et al. 2007; Salamon et al. 2008). Some nonprofits that receive government money worry about retribution for engaging in public policy matters; and many foundations do not support the advocacy activities undertaken by nonprofits and place restrictions on using grant funds for lobbying purposes.

For nonprofits to become more active participants in public policy, agency leaders, staff, board members, and volunteers need to understand the importance of public policy participation. Foundations and govern-ment also need to recognize and support the role of nonprofits in making public policy. Support should be given for capacity-building activities, such as training on lobbying restrictions under government grant rules, lobbying and advocacy restrictions under tax rules, how to be an effective advocate, and building internal organizational capacity. It has been suggested that simplifying the rules governing lobbying, advocacy, and voter education would also strengthen nonprofit policy participation (Bass et al. 2007; Berry and Arons 2005; Smucker 2005).

The Alliance for Justice, OMB Watch, the Center for Lobbying the Public Interest, and the Independent Sector provide valuable information on advocacy and lobbying.

Berry and Arons (2005), among others, pose the question, if labor unions, chambers of commerce, and other tax-exempt 501(c) organizations are permitted to lobby without restrictions and support candidates running for elective office, why the restrictions on independent sector organizations?

---

### Case 8.1. Defiance of IRS Rules: Religious Leaders Want to Endorse Political Candidates

On September 28, 2008, thirty-three pastors from around the county participated in Pulpit Freedom Sunday, an initiative by the Alliance Defense Fund (ADF) to challenge the Internal Revenue Code prohibition against religious organizations' and charities' supporting or opposing candidates for political office. The goal is to have the Johnson Amendment, the 1954 amendment to the IRC that prohibits nonprofit organizations from engaging in partisan electioneering, declared unconstitutional. Prior to 1954, the IRS allowed nonprofit organizations to endorse political candidates while remaining exempt from federal income taxes. The ADF was founded in 1994 by Christian conservatives, including James C. Dobson of Focus on the Family and William Bright, founder of Campus Crusade for Christ. According to the ADF, it will fight any attempt the IRS makes "to remove a church's tax-exempt status because a pastor exercised his constitutional right to engage in religious speech from the pulpit" (cited in OMB Watch 2008).

There is no consensus in the religious community. The chairman of the Interfaith Alliance board told the *Washington Post* that "a sanctuary should not be a place of political agitation on behalf of a candidate" (Associated Press 2009b). Two Ohio pastors asked clergy to preach about the benefit of the separation of church and state on September 21. The Ohio pastors led a group of fifty-five religious leaders who filed a complaint with the IRS asking the agency to force ADF to stop encouraging pastors to violate federal tax law on Pulpit Freedom Sunday.

Supporters of the ban believe that allowing electioneering churches to engage in partisan political activity would create a disparity between religious and nonreligious nonprofit organizations by giving religious organization groups greater speech rights. Opponents of the ban believe that the ban inhibits religious organizations' ability to speak about the moral and social issues of the day, even though the prohibition only applies to partisan support or opposition of a candidate, not issue advocacy. Americans United for Separation of Church and State has asked the IRS to investigate seven churches in which pastors violated the IRS rules on Pulpit Freedom Sunday. At this point in time, the pastors defying the order had not heard whether or not the IRS will take action against them.

*Sources:* Associated Press 2009b; Goodstein 2008; Merriam 2008; OMB Watch 2008; Sataline 2008a, 2008b; Slevin 2008; Vitello 2008.

---

### Case 8.2. Suing the Federal Government

The National Air Disaster Alliance Foundation sued the U.S. Department of Transportation (DOT) to adopt long-standing safety regulations. The complaint was filed in U.S. District Court in Washington. The group says the government is not improving air safety fast enough. The lawsuit seeks to force the government to approve safety measures recommended by the National Transportation Safety Board as far back as the 1990s. The suit accuses the DOT and the Federal Aviation Authority (FAA) of continuing to "shirk their duties to the traveling public" by not doing so.

*Source:* Associated Press 2009a.

---

### Case 8.3. A New Advocacy Group Calling Attention to Persons with Disabilities

In Broward County, Florida, there is an advocacy group dedicated to furthering the cause of the mentally disabled, managed by the people it aims to help. Its name is Abilities Venti, named after Starbucks, where the people who formed the foundation first met. Members are proud of their abilities, and "venti," the biggest coffee Starbucks offers, refers to large-scale talent. The nonprofit is only one year old and has forty members. Its members have various disabilities, including cerebral palsy, autism, and varying degrees of mental capacity. "Just because we have a disability doesn't mean we can't do a lot of things. That's the message we want to bring to the community," says Nick Stone, its president. Two social workers act as advisers to the group. Abilities Venti members have lobbied state lawmakers for funds in Tallahassee and their home offices. They volunteer, present workshops at conferences, and encourage employers to hire the disabled.

*Source:* Nolin 2009.

---

## References

Alliance for Justice (2007). About advocacy: Lobbying. July 16. www.afj.org/for-nonprofits-foundations/resources-and-publications/about-advocacy-lobbying.html.

Associated Press (2009a). Advocates sue to force air safety regulations. *St. Petersburg Times,* February 25, 3A.

———. (2009b). No word from I.R.S. on protest by pastors. *New York Times,* April 25, A19. www.nytimes.com/2009/04/26/us/politics/26churches.html.

Bass, G.D., D.F. Arons, K. Guinane, M.R. Carter, and S. Rees (2007). *Seen but not heard: Strengthening nonprofit advocacy.* Washington, DC: Aspen Institute.

Berry, J.M., and D.F. Arons (2005). *A voice for nonprofits.* Washington, DC: Brookings Institution Press.

Boris, E.T. (2006). Introduction. Nonprofit organizations in a democracy—roles and responsibilities. In *Nonprofits and government: Collaboration and conflict* (2nd ed.), ed. E.T. Boris and C.E. Steuerle, 1–35. Washington, DC: Urban Institute.

Dessingue, D. (2004). Politics and the pulpit: 2004. A guide to the Internal Revenue code restrictions on the political activity of religious organizations. September. Washington, DC: Pew Forum on Religion and Public Life. www.gcfa.org/PDFs/politicspulpit.pdf.

FitzGerald, E., & McNutt, J.G. (1999). Electronic advocacy in policy practice: A framework for teaching technologically based practice. *Journal of Social Work Education,* 35(3), 331–41.

Goodstein, L. (2008). Request for I.R.S. inquiry into pastors' endorsements. *New York Times,* October 4, A17.

Hessenius, B. (2007). *Hardball lobbying for nonprofits: Real advocacy for nonprofits in the new century.* New York: Palgrave Macmillan.

Hick, S.F., and J.G. McNutt (eds.) (2002). *Advocacy, activism, and the Internet: Community organization and social policy.* Chicago: Lyceum Books.

Independent Sector (2010). The basics of nonprofit advocacy. www.independentsector. org/the_basics_of_nonprofit_lobbying.
Internal Revenue Service (IRS) (2010a). Lobbying. June 11. www.irs.gov/charities/ article/0,,id=163392,00.html.
———. (2010b). Measuring lobbying: Substantial part test. June 14. www.irs.gov/ charities/article/0,,id=163393,00.html.
Merriam, J. (2008). Pastors to protest IRS rules on political advocacy: Interview with Robert W. Tuttle. September 19. Pew Forum. http://pewforum.org/Church-State-Law/Pastors-To-Protest-IRS-Rules-on-Political-Advocacy.aspx.
O'Connell, B. (1999). *Civil society: The underpinnings of American democracy.* Hanover, NH: University Press of New England.
OMB Watch (2008). Pastors challenge church electioneering ban. October 7. www. ombwatch.org/node/3808.
Nolin, Robert. (2009). Advocates for disabled united in common cause. *Sun-Sentinel* (Ft. Lauderdale, Florida), March 6. http://articles.sun-sentinel.com/2009–03–06/ news/0903050863_1_miniature-golf-tournament-civic-groups-members.
*Regan v. Taxation without Representation* (1983). 461 U.S. 540.
Salamon, L.M. (2002). The resilient sector: The state of nonprofit America. In *The state of nonprofit America,* ed. L.M. Salamon. Washington, DC: Brookings Institution Press.
Salamon, L.M., S.L. Geller, and S.C. Lorentz (2008). Nonprofit America: A force for democracy? Johns Hopkins University Center for Civil Society Studies. www. jhu.edu/listeningpost/news/pdf/advocacy9.pdf.
Sataline, S. (2008a). Pastors may defy IRS gag rule. *Wall Street Journal,* May 9, A5.
———. (2008b). Politics from pulpit will deliver challenges to IRS. *Wall Street Journal,* September 24, A12.
Slevin, P. (2008). Ban on political endorsements by pastors targeted. *Washington Post,* September 8, A03.
Smucker, B. (2005). Nonprofit lobbying. In *The Jossey-Bass handbook of nonprofit leadership and management* (2nd ed.), ed. Robert D. Herman and Associates, 230–53. San Francisco: Jossey-Bass.
Vitello, P. (2008). Pastors' Web electioneering attracts U.S. reviews of tax exemption. *New York Times,* September 3, B1.
Young, D.R. (2006). Complementary, supplementary, or adversarial? Nonprofit–government relations. In *Nonprofits and government: Collaboration and conflict* (2nd ed.), ed. E.T. Boris and C.E. Steuerle, 37–79. Washington, DC: Urban Institute.

# Epilogue

# Expectations for the Future

As noted throughout the book, nonprofit organizations are facing tough economic times. In the immediate future it looks like they will be confronted with less revenue to provide services and programs. We can expect that a decrease in funding for social services, health care, education, recreation, and arts and culture programs will continue. Instead of expanding programs, organizations are considering the elimination or reduction of some programs, reduced hours of operation, possible mergers with other agencies, and in some cases even shutting their doors. Nonprofits that survive will be required to have a comprehensive understanding of the environment in which they operate, which will require a greater understanding of the topics covered in this book.

Greater attention to ethical behavior and accountability is important. Capable board governance is required. Understanding public policy and intergovernmental relations will become more important, as will advocacy and lobbying activities to make sure that communities, funders, and elected officials understand the contributions that nonprofits make to society. Nonprofits will need improved financial management systems and oversight of their financial activities, and will also need to investigate realistic strategies for diversifying their sources of revenue. With greater competition for revenues and resources, attention to performance outcomes is likely to be increased. Government funders, individual donors, foundations, and volunteers will likely invest their time and money with nonprofits that can substantiate their program and mission achievements and with which they have developed trusted relationships.

Nonprofits are also facing leadership challenges. The ranks of nonprofit executive directors will diminish when the baby boomers retire, but that is also an opportunity to recruit new leaders with different skill sets. It provides an opportunity to evaluate whether the variety of demographics located within the community is reflected in the board of directors and the agency staff.

To meet the present challenges and plan for the future, nonprofit administrators must understand the context and environment in which nonprofit organizations operate and provide leadership in defining public issues and developing solutions.

# Name Index

# Subject Index

# About the Author

**Joan E. Pynes** is a professor of public administration and director of the raduate certificate in nonprofit management at the University of South Florida. She is the author or coauthor of four books, most recently *Human Resources Management for Public and Nonprofit Organizations*, 3rd ed. (2009) and *Human Resources Management for Health Care Organizations: A Strategic Approach* (forthcoming). She is also the author or coauthor of more than fifty academic articles, book chapters, technical reports, and encyclopedia entries about public and nonprofit human resources management.